Politics of Pressure

Politics of Pressure

The Art of Lobbying

by
Malcolm Davies

· BRITISH BROADCASTING CORPORATION

Acknowledgment is due to the following for the use of photographs:
CHARLES BARKER WATNEY & POWELL page 101 (top); CAMERA PRESS
pages 94 (Bob Penn), 96 (Colin Davey), 97 (Cosmo Verner) and 103;
CONSUMERS' ASSOCIATION page 100 (top); MICHAEL DAUBE page 101
(bottom); MALCOLM DAVIES pages 90 and 95; GLC page 91; GREENPEACE
page 102 (top); MIKE HUSKISSON page 92 (bottom); THE LAW SOCIETY'S
GAZETTE page 100 (bottom); LEAGUE AGAINST CRUEL SPORTS page 92
(top); NATIONAL CONSUMER COUNCIL page 88; NATIONAL VIEWERS' &
LISTENERS' ASSOCIATION page 99 (top); PHOTO SOURCE pages 98 and 99
(bottom); PRESS ASSOCIATION pages 89 and 93.

Acknowledgment is also due to the following:
HAMISH HAMILTON LTD for the extract from *Peter Hall's Diaries* (1983, ed.
Goodwin, hardback and paperback editions) used by kind permission of
Sir Peter Hall; also for the extract from *The Diaries of a Cabinet Minister* by
Richard Crossman (1975–77, 3 vols, ed. Howard), co-published with
Jonathan Cape.

The extracts from the letters from *The Times* are reproduced by kind
permission of Professor Goehr and Mr Burton.

This book is published in conjunction with the
BBC Continuing Education Television series
Politics of Pressure, first broadcast on BBC 1 from
February 1985.

The series is produced by Tony Roberts

Acknowledgment is due to Derek Matthews for the cover illustration

Published to accompany a series of programmes prepared in
consultation with the BBC Continuing Education
Advisory Council

First published 1985
Published by the British Broadcasting Corporation,
35 Marylebone High Street, London W1M 4AA

Typeset in Linotron 11/12pt Baskerville and printed in England at
The Pitman Press, Bath, Avon
Cover printed by Belmont Press, Northampton

ISBN 0 563 21105 9

Contents

Acknowledgements

I am indebted to a number of people who helped in the production of this book. They include Jennie Allen, Colleen Lewis, Michael Molyneux, Simon Molyneux and Tim Scott. A special thanks goes to Tony Roberts, producer of the BBC TV series *Politics of Pressure* who spent much time deciphering my writing. I would also like to record my appreciation of the thought which went into the contributions of those interviewed for the book and TV series. A list of those interviewed can be found after the Introduction. I am grateful to Mike Daube for permission to use his unpublished material. By the summer of 1984 the manuscript had become so much a part of everyday life that we took it on our family holiday to the Dordogne. For this intrusion into domestic life I apologise to Pamela, Adam, Nicholas and Oliver.

Malcolm Davies
15 October 1984

Introduction

Influencing government: lobbying and British politics

This book is about political influence. Not the political
influence exercised by professional politicians, bureaucrats
and party officials who form part of the official elements of
government, nor that exercised by press barons and media
producers whose influence is felt by the way they represent
issues and so shape the dialogue of politics. It is about those
organisations that make up the lobby interests, which,
although they have no recognised official status in the
British Constitution, undoubtedly help to influence
political decisions. When manifesto commitments are vague
or government policy undeveloped, the pressure of lobby
interests will play a part in identifying and defining problems in society and providing solutions to these problems.

In essence this is an introductory book about the organisations, processes, techniques and consequences of political
lobbying in so far as they effect central government in
Britain. The stimulus to write such a book was provided by
the BBC Television series *Politics of Pressure*. The book, like
the five programmes in the series, is aimed at a general
audience interested in British politics.

Most of the quoted material in the book results from
original interviews held in the course of making the television series. Interviews were held with over 30 MPs, ex-civil
servants and organisers or representatives of the many
pressure and interest groups who engage in lobbying. The
book provides the opportunity to give lengthier extracts of
those interviews than appear in the television programmes
and, whenever possible, I have allowed the interviewees
the chance to describe and explain the nature of lobbying in their own words. A list of contributing persons
and organisations is provided at the end of this introduction.

The book is organised into five chapters which examine
similar themes to each of the five television programmes.

It contains interview material from lobbyists, politicians and government officials concerned with five areas of political lobbying: 'moral issues'; the 'use of the countryside'; consumer and legal interests; penal policy; and the world of the arts. The intention of the book is not only to describe some of the organisations and activities of lobby groups within the five defined areas of political interest, but to make general points about the nature of lobbying and its part in the British political system.

Chapter 1 looks at some of the personalities associated with lobbying in Britain and how lobby groups became established; also the development of lobbying since the end of the Second World War, and the contribution that pressure groups can make to the democratic process.

Chapter 2 considers three different views of the nature of political democracy, Burkean, corporatist and pluralist, and assesses the part pressure groups can play in each. The organisational styles of differing pressure groups specifically concerned with the use of the countryside are also examined in this chapter.

Chapter 3 concentrates on the part that Parliament plays in the lobbying process and assesses whether or not it provides the best target for pressure group activity. The private Member's bill, sponsored by the Consumers' Association to end the solicitors' monopoly on conveyancing, is discussed in this chapter.

Chapter 4 looks at pressure points outside Westminster, such as Whitehall, Strasbourg and the political party organisations, and the use of the courts as a lobby strategy.

Chapter 5 looks at the part played by the media in representing pressure groups and issues, and also provides an assessment of the pressure groups' role as guarantors of political democracy. The focus in this chapter is on the arts and the controversies surrounding the Arts Council's funding policy.

The term lobbying derives from American politics. It originally described the attempts to exert influence or pressure on elected representatives in Congress. Although an established and recognised practice in Washington by 1832, the term did not enter British politics in this sense (according to the Oxford English Dictionary) until 1859.

At Westminster the word 'lobby' has three other possible

meanings. The large entrance hall known as the Central Lobby is the place where members of the public may meet MPs; it is the collective name for the press correspondents on parliamentary matters; and it is the corridor into which MPs go when they are voting in a division. Conservative MP and journalist Julian Critchley explains the differing meanings of the term:

> 'The first meaning is architectural. There is a large room which is the Members' Lobby which is restricted to Members of Parliament. Then there are the lobby correspondents of national newspapers who lurk and wait for us. There is also the Central Lobby which is the sort of crossroads of the Palace of Westminster and that is where the electorate can come, providing they have the name of a Member of Parliament whom they wish to see, and providing they are prepared to be stripped and searched by security people. The word 'lobbying' of course has its origins in the Central Lobby and Members' Lobby of the House of Commons.'

But it is, of course, another meaning of the term 'lobby' which provides the central theme of this book. The constitutional writer Lord Bryce wrote in 1888 that 'lobby' referred to: 'Persons not being members of the legislature who undertake to influence its members and thereby secure the passing of Bills.' Today the activity of lobbyists is broader than recognised by Bryce, as it is not merely directed at the legislature. Whitehall and Strasbourg, as well as Blackpool and Brighton during the party conference season, are just as likely venues for lobbying in the 1980s. Nor is it at the elected representative at Westminster that lobbyists direct all their energies. They may think it more effective to persuade, amongst others, civil servants, members of the executive, local government officials, or the electorate at large.

To reflect today's realities a further amendment should be made to Bryce's definition; it is rarely 'persons' as individuals, but organised groups of individuals who undertake the great bulk of lobbying activity.

Professor S. E. Finer's definition of 'the lobby' is the one which encompasses the range of activities examined in this book:

> 'The sum of organisations in so far as they are occupied

at any point in time trying to influence the policy of public bodies in their chosen direction, though (unlike political parties) never themselves prepared to undertake the direct government of the country.'

To be considered a part of the process of lobbying in British politics, a group must have the following characteristics:

1   An organisation.
2   A recognisable and definable group of individuals who have a shared set of interests or attitudes.
3   A set of identifiable goals or articulated demands.
4   A purposeful strategy to influence the policy decisions of the executive, legislative or the judicial branch of government in Britain.

In writing a book about lobbying it is necessary to provide a definition of the organisations that are to be included. To do this I consulted two academic writers who have published books recently on this topic.

Dr Geoffrey Alderman's book *Pressure Groups and Government in Britain* was published in 1984. He prefers the generic term 'pressure group' to cover the range of groups involved in lobbying. He told me: 'I think we should interpret the term "pressure" in the broadest sense. I would distinguish two types of pressure groups. There are those who represent sectional "interests" that want to advance the interest of their own members. There are those who are interested in advancing particular causes.' An over-emphasis on definitional matters can be self-defeating, however, and he made the caveat that: 'There has been a great deal of misplaced academic endeavour in erecting typologies of pressure groups.' Dr Alderman does not like the word 'lobbying'. As a term which evolved in the United States to describe a particular activity that went on in the Congress, he feels it to be inapplicable to the context of Westminster and Whitehall.

Philip Lowe, who with Jane Goyder wrote *Environmental Groups in Politics*, published in 1983, explained why they preferred not to use Dr Alderman's favoured term 'pressure group':

'We wanted to get away from the category of pressure group because we felt it has a lot of negative connotations. It is used in the press and by politicians in an evaluatory sense and has the connotation that groups with that label are not legitimate.'

In my experience, MPs who take a Burkean view of their role as representatives (see Chapter 2) certainly do seem to feel hostility towards pressure groups, as Philip Lowe suggests. But I also prefer not to use the term 'pressure group' as a generic concept, as I think it better describes those functionally specific organisations which are established exclusively for political ends, such as Shelter or CND, and therefore excludes organisations such as the Roman Catholic Church, the Rotary Club, the British Medical Association, the British Olympics Committee, the National Institute for the Deaf, the Spastics Society and the Transport and General Workers' Union. All these are groups which were established for non-political purposes but which to differing degrees engage in the activity of political lobbying from time to time. Hence I differ from Dr Alderman, not only in this, but also in seeing an advantage in using the imported American phrase 'lobby groups' as it is more comprehensive than the concept of pressure or interest group.

Furthermore, I feel it is time that we recognised that the nineteenth- and early twentieth-century distinction between American and British politics is no longer so valid, especially with the evolution of American-style lobby activities into the albeit begrudging and disapproving world of Westminster. In short, lobbying is now a British phenomenon.

Julian Critchley agrees that we are 'slowly and gradually' moving towards a more American style of politics:

> 'Americans in recent years have gone in for what is called single-issue politics, which is self-explanatory, and here we are starting to get the same sort of phenomenon . . . A group of people, for instance the environmentalists, or the Campaign for Nuclear Disarmament, or the anti-vivisection lobby, get together on a national basis and make the lives of Members of Parliament a misery in order to try to achieve their particular objectives.'

This meaning of the term 'lobby' is now well established in Britain. It is to be found in the newspapers that report on politics and is used in Parliament. The Minister for

Information Technology, Mr Kenneth Baker, explained to the House of Commons on 19 July 1984 why he had not yet decided whether or not to impose a levy on blank video cassettes to be used as a source for funding the film industry with the words: 'It is an issue which evokes strong feelings on both sides. One lobby is totally opposed to a levy on blank tapes: that is, the consumers.'

The literature on lobbying identifies three basic categories of organisations: the pressure group, the interest group and the voluntary association. I define these as follows:

Pressure groups   Principle, cause or promotional organisations. These are single-issue, politically specific organisations which are concerned with the promotion of policies derived from a shared set of values, beliefs or ideology, eg the Howard League for Penal Reform, the Child Poverty Action Group. These groups often develop with, or have their roots in, charitable organisations.

Interest groups   Protectional groups. These are based on multi-functional organisations such as trade unions and professional associations which have a common economic interest.

Non-economic and non-political voluntary associations   Based on social groups and groupings such as ramblers, boy scouts, anglers and Anglicans, these engage less regularly in political lobbying as their primary function is neither to protect nor promote.

Although I have adopted a broad definition of lobbying, my intention is not to include all forms of political influence. This book will only examine lobbying in the public arena and ignore efforts to solicit powerful private bodies, such as multi-national corporations. Even in the public sector, there must be omissions: I shall not be concerned with lobbying at local government level, for example, but will concentrate on the politics of central government. Also excluded in this account of lobbying are the individual efforts of citizens or constituents to persuade or cajole ministers or their MP. Instead I have focussed on lobbying where it involves an intermediate organisation between a citizen and the Government. Lobbying must be an influence that is actively sought, rather than achieved by inertia or accident.

Finally, the focus of this book will be on attempts to influence the policy level of public decisions and not those which seek to effect the execution of policy. For example, it will not seek to examine the way entrepreneurs and manufacturers like De Lorean set out to win government contracts. Some might regard this as a serious omission, but I do not pretend this is to be an exhaustive and comprehensive study of all forms of political influence. I hope simply that it will help to illuminate one small part of the total picture of power in contemporary Britain.

Apart from Bryce's comments, there is a curious lack of reference to political lobbying in the work of British constitutional historians – and indeed in contemporary constitutional law courses. Edward Porritt's book *The Unreformed House of Commons: Parliamentary Representation Before 1832*, published in 1902, may be forgiven for it deals with a period in parliamentary affairs when the term 'lobby' referred solely to the hallways where division votes were to be counted. But *Abraham and Hawtrey's Parliamentary Dictionary*, the third edition of which was published in 1970 and edited by Hawtrey and Barclay, has no comments whatsoever about lobbying. Even the revered bible of parliamentary procedure *Erskine May's Parliamentary Practice*, which in 1983 was in its 20th edition and had been edited and revised by no less an authority than Sir Charles Gordon, the long-standing Clerk of the House of Commons, makes no mention of the word 'lobby' other than as the corridor where MPs vote.

How unlike equivalent works of reference about the American Congress. The latest *Guide to Congress*, published by the Congressional Quarterly (2nd edition, 1976), refers to lobbying in the 'Glossary of Congressional Terms' at the very beginning of the book and points out that the business of lobbying is based on the First Amendment to the Constitution which declares that Congress shall make no laws abridging the right of the people 'to petition the government for a redress of grievances'. It is not only the constitutional recognition of lobbying but also its political reality which is recognised more readily in America. The *Guide to Congress* contains a whole section entitled 'Pressure on Congress' and a chapter devoted to 'Lobbying'.

The advantages of lobbying in a democracy are spelled out in the *Guide to Congress*.

'It is widely recognised that pressure groups, whether operating through general campaigns designed to sway public opinion or through direct contacts with members of Congress, perform some important and indispensable functions. Such functions include helping to inform both Congress and the public about problems and issues, stimulating public debate, opening a path to Congress for the wronged and needy, and making known to Congress the practical aspects of proposed legislation – whom it would help, whom it would hurt, who is for it and who against it.'

As Senator for Massachussets in 1956, John Kennedy elaborated on the *raison d'être* of the lobbyist:

'As expert technicians . . . they . . . are capable of explaining complex and difficult subjects in a clear, understandable fashion . . . they . . . prepare briefs, memoranda, legislative analysis and draft legislation . . . they frequently can provide useful statistics and information not otherwise available.' ('To Keep the Lobbyist Within Bounds', *New York Times Magazine*, Feb 1956).

The *Guide to Congress* also refers to the potential disadvantages of a system of organised lobbying:

'Pressure groups are apt to lead Congress into decisions which benefit the pressure group but do not necessarily serve other parts of the public. A group's power to influence legislation is more often based on its arguments than on the size of its membership, the amount of financial and manpower resources it can commit to a legislative pressure campaign and the astuteness of its representatives.'

It was not fear of distorting the democratic process so much as fear of corruption by less than honourable – and bribable – representatives that led Congress to regulate the activity of the lobby. In 1946 The Federal Regulation of Lobbying Act was passed, which required lobbyists to register and report on their activities, its predominant aim being to curb dishonest practices. The significance of this Act for the American political process is illuminated by the fact that legal cases about lobbying have been pursued to the level of the Supreme Court.

Despite the lack of comment about lobbying and pressure groups in British constitutional textbooks and parliamentary guides, there are those who regard the role of pressure groups as crucial for democracy and an effective source of power in our society. Those who subscribe to this view are termed 'pluralists'.

Pluralism, as a theory of power, attributes to voluntary associations, pressure groups and interest groups a key role in the establishment and maintenance of democracy; as an intermediate layer between the citizen and the state, they provide a source of effective resistance to the otherwise all-embracing power of the modern state. Furthermore, the pluralists argue, democracy is strengthened by providing an additional focus for political mobilisation other than political parties. As a form of participation they can be more relevant to the immediate demands of sections of society because they do not need to make their appeal to such diverse audiences as political parties. Not constrained by the need to appeal broadly to the ritualistic conflicts associated with elections, they can respond more flexibly to the contingent events that provide part of the agenda of politics. They can mobilise groups of individuals around specific issues and attitudes.

I will be looking at how valid the pluralists' view is in more detail later on in the book and also at a range of other questions about lobbying and democracy. For example, do pressure and interest groups shore up or distort the democratic process? Do they provide alternative means of political participation? Are they just another bureaucratic and distant political reality, as remote and alienating for the individual as other parts of the political system? Are they as crucial in defining power as the pluralists claim? The fear that lobbying can distort the democratic process is advanced by those who are steeped in the traditions of parliamentary government with its roots in the elitist and consensual view of politics as embodied in Edmund Burke's view of Parliament.

Not only will I be looking at questions about the consequences for democracy of lobbying, but also the techniques and processes involved in the organised efforts, and the strategies and tactics open to a pressure group: campaigning, demonstrating, negotiating, infiltrating, seducing, harrying, convincing, soliciting, blackmailing, bribing, informing and misinforming. The strategy of the lobbyist is concerned not only with a broad appeal to the electoral grass-roots and submissions to elected local or national representatives, but also with representations specifically focused on administrators and politicians who form the Government.

Some groups, like the Animal Liberation Front, prefer direct action and are prepared to use violence. Ten thousand elderly citizens, on the other hand, opted to attend a peaceful rally at County Hall in London (in support of the Pensioners' Action Day) on 29 September 1983. One month after the rally more than two million people took part in a series of co-ordinated demonstrations against nuclear weapons throughout Europe. The oil industry prefers to misinform: in September 1983 *The Sunday Times* reported that the oil industry had misled the Government during private consultation earlier that year by not revealing the existence of a refinery in Britain which could already produce lead-free petrol suitable for all cars. The Government's acceptance of the continued use of lead in petrol until the next century was based on the oil industry's claim that it would cost too much to produce lead-free petrol for both old and new cars, and that a long phasing-out period was essential on economic grounds.

What factors determine the strategies chosen? Basically it is a case of internal organisational factors, the external political context within which the groups operate, and the inter-relationship between these two.

The internal organisation features of lobby groups can be analysed in terms of quantitative and qualitative factors. The quantitative factors are:

1   Resources (money and manpower).
2   Size and scope (how many employees, how many offices, how wide a network of contacts and organisers).

The qualitative factors are:

1   Clarity and singleness of purpose.
2   Commitment of membership and leadership to this purpose.
3   The level of cohesion within the organisation and the consequences of internal divisions.
4   The effectiveness and astuteness of organisational leaders and representatives.
5   Organisational efficiency.

6   The willingness of the leadership and the membership to adopt alternative strategies and tactics when necessary, and the extent to which this may involve illicit, illegal, or illegitimate methods of lobbying.

An examination of these internal features of an organisation concerned with lobbying alone is insufficient if we wish to understand the impact that it can have on decisions made by the Government. Lobbying does not take place in a political, economic and cultural vacuum. As David Truman, an American academic who wrote the influential pluralist book *The Governmental Process*, points out, there is a need for pressure groups to operate with cohesive and appropriate organisations relevant to the governmental form. But it is not only the form of government – in terms of the system of elections and the relationship between the executive and legislative branches of government – which provides the context in which lobbies operate. There are also economic constraints which impose practical limitations on what can be achieved; as can the less concrete but no less real ideological and cultural factors which help to shape our political demands and define our notions of the legitimate and the desirable, and deflect our vision from what we conceive to be impractical, unethical and impossible.

In any political system, there are two basic types of constraint which an effective lobby group must heed. Firstly, there are those which result from the socio-economic structures of society with its in-built prejudices and taken-for-granted practices that underpin everyday life. These prejudices and practices involve the system of production and its corresponding interests, which, because of their strategic significance in the economy, are unlikely to be challenged or even questioned by normal lobbying techniques. These socio-economic interests are not static; change can occur in a number of ways, not least through technological innovation. This frequently has ramifications for protectional interest groups.

The second fundamental constraint emanates from the political process within which lobbying operates. Four factors are relevant: a group's access to the decision-makers; ideological factors; the system of elections; and a group's relationship with other agencies and lobby groups.

Some groups have ready access to the political decision-makers. They enjoy a privileged relationship with government. They have been incorporated into the decision-making process, or have been granted a deliberate representational monopoly. Some groups are seen to have the status of playing a legitimate role in policy formation. The most influential receive unsolicited notice of policy discussions at which their attendance is automatic and their advice is listened to with deference. Access will be affected by the ideological concurrence between the Government and the lobby groups concerned. Sometimes it will be established by the permanent officials in a government department rather than by the minister. Regular negotiations over a long period establish a group's position so that it becomes, in the eyes of a department, the natural expression and representative of a given sectional interest.

Formal liaison between the Government and such lobby organisations is established for consultative discussion and inquiries. This 'insider status' of certain organisations is revealed by the way in which they almost automatically have their views included in submissions of evidence to a Royal Commission. Officials should consult all relevant organisations, but in practice not all lobby groups will acquire this official recognition; some will be excluded from the consultative process. Having achieved 'insider status' a lobby group might prefer a strategy of quiet diplomacy to one of 'going public' with issues. Insider groups have a stake in not disrupting cosy relationships with the Government or provoking counter-mobilisation by other groups, which might be awakened by the sound of public controversy.

Finally, access might result from a group's position in a political party, for example as part of the coalition of interests established within the party of government. For years the farming lobby could count on the Minister of Agriculture being part of any Tory Cabinet and have ready access to the department. In similar fashion the TUC could count on the Department of Labour, now the Department of Employment, being more receptive to its overtures during a period of Labour government.

Ideology is a crucial variable determining not only a lobby group's commitments but also its chances of success. Ideology as a system of ideas, which is related to a manner of thinking and practice in a sector of society, can appeal to the wider electorate where it is perceived as consistent with, or even speaking out for, popular latent values. Where a group's ideology is sympathetic to or supportive of party, government or bureaucratic policy then the group will more readily be granted access to, and possible incorporation into, key decision-making bodies.

Some groups gain respectability in the eyes of a government department. M. Ryan in *The Acceptable Pressure Group* contrasts the legitimacy granted to the Howard League by the Home Office, regardless of the party in power, and the outsider status of Radical Alternatives to Prison (RAP).

Lobbying techniques will be directly affected by the system of elections when groups aim their appeal at the electorate. In Britain the lobby group Aims of Industry spends thousands of pounds on advertisements at general election time in the hope of reminding the electorate of the need to promote free enterprise by voting Conservative. In the USA many larger lobby groups single out sympathetic candidates for their endorsement. In California, lobby groups have been able to change the law on the punishment of criminals and alter the level of state taxation through their success at public initiatives – what we would call referendums – which are binding on the state government.

The system of elections can have a less direct influence on government policy than is found to be the case in California, and this too can affect the role that lobby groups play. The British system of parliamentary government sets up very little separation of powers between the legislature and the executive. The election of parliamentary representatives also serves to establish the party of government. Government controls Parliament through the party whips in the House of Commons. This can mean that lobby groups by-pass Parliament and aim instead to influence party policy, or lobby the executive branch of government directly.

Ironically, it can have just the alternative effect when the Government is fearful of unpopular or controversial issues, as happened with the parliamentary votes on the abolition and, later, the restoration of capital punishment. A sudden coyness results in the absence of a government line on an issue. The whips are left dangling as the House of Commons is permitted a free vote. At this point MPS come into their own as the major target for lobby group activity.

Today, a similar campaign would more probably start with one of the growing number of specialist consultancy firms concerned with the business of political lobbying. Their expertise can be used for advice about an advertising campaign aimed at the public. What Saatchi and Saatchi did for the Conservative Party they could do again for a lobby group. Specialist firms contract MPS to act as spokesmen or women for a cause. MPS can be hired to represent not their constituents but any organisation that can foot the bill.

A group's success will also be affected by its relationship with other lobby groups and allied agencies. Some groups enter into coalition with a number of like-minded groups to form an umbrella organisation, such as The 1984 Campaign for Freedom of Information. This is made up of 14 supporting organisations which include the Patients' Association, the Legal Action Group, the National Union of Journalists, Friends of the Earth and Shelter. In addition, there is a long list of other groups and personalities associated with the campaign, which reads like a pressure group's *Who's Who*. Des Wilson, born in New Zealand, is the chairman; he has previously been the Director of Shelter, Chairman of The Campaign for Lead Free Air (CLEAR), is currently Chairman of the Board of Directors of the Friends of the Earth, and a member of the executive committees of the Child Poverty Action Group, National Council for Civil Liberties and the Green Alliance. Ralph Nader, the famous American lobbyist, is an international adviser to the Campaign for Freedom of Information.

Another American, Larry Gostin, formerly the Legal Director for MIND, became the General Secretary of the National Campaign for Civil Liberties (NCCL) in 1983. Indeed the world of post-1960s British pressure groups does seem a bit incestuous. For example, Ruth Lister, who worked for the Council for One Parent Families, then moved to become the Director of the Child Poverty Action Group (CPAG). Undoubtedly these people have the relevant experience and forceful personalities required to run a successful pressure group, but the trend also indicates the existence of a professional career structure in politics which is an alternative to that offered by the House of Commons.

It is doubtful whether umbrella organisations can work effectively over a long period, other than by playing a generalised role as an information forum. Umbrella groups like the Trades Union Congress and the Confederation of British Industry have little internal cohesion because of divergent interests amongst the constituent member groups. They have few consistent policy demands and they have regularly failed to deliver the support of those constituent groups for policy agreements negotiated with the Government.

A group's relationship with other lobby groups is not necessarily harmonious – either because it represents opposing interests or views, or because they are all seeking funds from the limited resources of central government expenditure.

Political systems are rarely static and the formation of one lobby group is likely to create wave-like disturbances which can lead to counter-mobilisation. As the American Professor of Sociology, A. Etzioni, puts it in *The Active Society* (1968): 'A universal problem of mobilising units is finding modes of mobilisation that will trigger off as little counter-mobilisation as possible.'

As I pointed out earlier, the definition of the lobby provided by Bryce in 1888 is in need of revision if it is to convey the wider range of activities that pass for lobbying today. The political process in Britain has changed sufficiently to render Bryce's exclusive focus on the legislature an anachronism, reflecting a view of a period when Parliament was more worthy of the lobbyists' attention. A more accurate conception of lobbying in the 1980s would have to take account of three developments in the twentieth century which have altered the context of lobbying. They are: the dwindling power of Parliament and the corresponding increase in the power of the executive branch of government in Whitehall; the growth since the Second World War of a corporatist state; and the growth in the 1960s of pluralism, when all types of groups became politicised and demanded involvement in government decisions.

The dwindling power of Parliament was a consequence of several factors: the growth and complexity of government; the reorganisation after 1918 of political parties seeking a mass mandate; the central role of political leadership reinforced by the use of the mass media in political campaigning by the parties; and the loss of international political independence as Britain increasingly became the slave of world events rather than the country which ruled the waves. As the Empire disappeared there emerged a world shaped by international markets, defence pacts and multinational corporations. The British State's sovereignty was eroded by membership of the International Monetary Fund, NATO, and, the final straw, by the activities of the European Economic Community in Strasbourg.

The decline in the relative importance of Parliament has three consequences for lobby groups. Some turned their attention to lobbying the executive; greater complexity and scope of government meant that much of the work of government was hidden from parliamentary scrutiny; it made sense to lobby directly the officials who were making the decisions. Other groups, recognising the importance of the party election manifestos as a source of political initiative for a new Government, sought to influence the decision-making process within a particular party, whether at conference, on the National Executive Committee, or by getting acquiescent candidates endorsed. Both CND and the animal campaigners were successful in the Labour Party; their views were taken up as party policy and included in the election manifestos of 1979 and 1983. The third consequence was that lobby groups adopted a more internationalist strategy and forged links with consumer groups or peace movements in Europe and America.

List of people interviewed

Dr Geoffrey Alderman, Lecturer at Royal Holloway College, and author of *Pressure Groups and Government in Great Britain* (1984)

Bryan Appleyard, Arts Correspondent of *The Times*, and author of *The Culture Club: Crisis in the Arts* (1984)

David Astor, Chairman of the Council for the Protection of Rural England

Bill Baggs, Hart District Councillor and Hands Off Hook Action Group

Patrick Cormack, Conservative MP for Staffordshire South, Joint Chairman of the all-party Heritage Group and Chairman of the Conservative Arts and Heritage Committee in Parliament, Member of the Historic Buildings Council

Richard Course, Director of the League against Cruel Sports

Julian Critchley, Conservative MP for Aldershot, writer, journalist and broadcaster

Sir Charles Cunningham, Permanent Secretary at the Home Office 1957–1966

Mike Daube, adviser to Action on Alcohol Abuse and former Director of ASH

Peter Duckworth, Chairman, Hart District Council

Nicholas Fairbairn, Conservative MP for Perth and Kinross, QC, poet, author, painter, former Chairman of the Scottish Society for the Defence of Literature and Member of the Edinburgh Festival Committee, Solicitor-General for Scotland 1979–82

Frank Field, Labour MP for Birkenhead and former director of the Child Poverty Action Group 1969–79

Bryan Forbes, film actor, writer and director, Managing Director and Chief Executive of EMI-MGM 1969–71, Writers' Guild of Great Britain, President of National Youth Theatre

Larry Gostin, General Secretary of the National Council for Civil Liberties, former Director of MIND 1974–83 (the National Association for Mental Health), first winner in

1982 of the Rosemary Delbridge Memorial Award for his contribution to pressure group politics

Robin Grove-White, Director of the Council for the Protection of Rural England

Ole Hansen, Director of the Legal Action Group

Sir Christopher Hewetson, President of the Law Society 1983–84

Hilary Jackson, Co-ordinator of the Abortion Law Reform Association

Dave Leadbetter, Inquest (a pressure group for the reform of coroner's courts)

Ken Livingstone, Leader of the Greater London Council

Philip Lowe, The Bartlett School of Architecture and Planning, University College, University of London, co-author with J. Goyder of *Environmental Groups in Politics* (1983)

Austin Mitchell, Labour MP for Grimsby who introduced the House Buyers Bill in 1983

David Myles, ex-Conservative MP for Banff, Convenor for Scottish NFU and tenant farmer

Sir Henry Plumb, President of the NFU 1970–1979, Conservative Member of the European Parliament and Chairman of the Agricultural Committee of the European Parliament 1979–82

Geoffrey Robinson, Labour MP for Coventry NW, former Chief Executive of Jaguar Cars and Triumph Motorcycles (Meriden) Ltd

Andrew Roth, Parliamentary Profiles Services Ltd, author of *The Business Backgrounds of Members of Parliament*

Michael Schofield, National Council for Civil Liberties, Campaign against Censorship, Abortion Law Reform, Campaign for Homosexual Equality, Cannabis Law Reform

Charles Secret, Friends of the Earth

Francis Sitwell, professional lobbyist with Roland Freeman Ltd working on the 'Save the GLC' campaign

Evie Soames, parliamentary consultant, Joint Managing Director of Charles Barker Watney and Powell

David Tench, Consumers' Association

Tony Ward, Inquest

Mary Whitehouse, President of the National Viewers' and Listeners' Association

Des Wilson, former Director of Shelter (the National Campaign for the Homeless) from 1966–71, former member of the National Executive of the CPAG and the National Council for Civil Liberties. In 1982 launched CLEAR (Campaign for Lead Free Air). In 1982 became the Chairman of the British Friends of the Earth. In 1984, as Chairman, launched the 1984 Committee for the Freedom of Information. Author of *Pressure: the A to Z of Campaigning in Britain* (1984)

Lord Young of Dartington, founder of the Consumers' Association, the Open University, the National Extension College, and the first Chairman of the Social Science Research Council 1965–68

Abbreviations used in the text

AAA	Action on Alcohol Abuse
ALRA	Abortion Law Reform Association
ASH	Action on Smoking and Health
CLA	Country Landowners' Association
CLEAR	Campaign for Lead-Free Air
CPAG	Child Poverty Action Group
CPRE	Council for the Protection of Rural England
CND	Campaign for Nuclear Disarmament
FOE	Friends of the Earth
HBF	Housebuilders' Federation
LACS	League Against Cruel Sports
LAG	Legal Action Group
MIND	National Association for Mental Health
NCCL	National Council for Civil Liberties
NFU	National Farmers' Union
NVALA	National Viewers' and Listeners' Association
RAP	Radical Alternatives to Prison
Shelter	National Campaign for the Homeless
SPUC	Society for the Protection of the Unborn Child

1 *Living with the Lobbyists*

1.1 *Celebrated lobbyists*

Both Des Wilson and Michael Young (now Lord Young of Dartington) were committed to active political involvement in the Labour Party before they launched out to pioneer new movements in British political history. With very different styles they have helped to shape the contours of political debate by providing alternatives to the traditional patterns of British politics, one in which the Labour and the Conservative Parties held a monopoly on the struggle for power. The venue for this was mainly Westminster, although occasionally also to be found on tour at Blackpool or Brighton.

Des Wilson now runs the Freedom of Information Campaign out of a tiny, two-roomed, top-floor office in King's Cross – an area favoured by many of the more radical pressure groups, such as the Legal Action Group and the Abortion Law Reform Association. You would think, given the high media profile achieved by Wilson, that he would have a whole building and a corps of staff. Instead there is one harrassed secretary/telephonist who occupies the other slit-trench-sized room in the offices of the Campaign for Freedom of Information.

But Des Wilson doesn't need large offices. A dynamic, shrewd judge of the British political system, he knows how to exploit the channels of communication and the functional inter-dependence that exists between the politicians and the media. His track record of campaigning successes since he left the Labour Party illustrates this point and would certainly enable him to win the Bell's Whisky Political Campaigner of the Decade Award.

In the 1960s Des Wilson was a member of the Labour Party and saw himself as part of the Kennedy generation. He became disillusioned with Harold Wilson's Labour Government and got involved with Shelter (the National Campaign for the Homeless), acting as Director from the late 1960s until 1971. During that time he was on the committee of the Child Poverty Action Group and the executive of the National Council for Civil Liberties, and also wrote a weekly campaigning column for the *Observer* newspaper. More recently he became involved with CLEAR (the Campaign for Lead Free Air), of which he is now Chairman, as he is also of the Friends of the Earth and The 1984 Campaign for Freedom of Information.

Des Wilson's career has brought him a degree of notoriety. He is a pressure group celebrity. In contrast, how many students of the Open University, or the National Extension College, or recipients of SSRC grants, or subscribers to *Which?* would recognise the face of Michael Young who did much to set up these institutions as a part of British life? 'A low-profile Sidney Webb' is one description applied to this pioneer of ideas and engineer of social institutions in Britain during the 1950s and '60s.

A Labour Party member from 1934 to 1981, Young became Secretary of the Policy Committee of the Labour Party in 1945. When considering new policy proposals for the 1950 election, the idea of a Consumers' Advice Centre, run as a government body, was suggested. In a Gallup poll survey on the Labour Party's election programme it was this idea which came out as the most popular amongst voters, and Young kept it in mind.

Some years later the time seemed right for it to resurface and, with the help of American friends, the Goodmans, he helped to form a committee which led to the production of the first issue of *Which?* in 1956. They held a press conference at the Waldorf Hotel which was attended by 200 journalists, but only *The Times* wrote about the event. At that time the press in general believed they were dealing with potentially litigious material and felt sure that law suits from the companies whose products had been criticised would follow shortly.

But the one paragraph in *The Times* led immediately to 5000 subscribers and enquiries in the first week. The day after the launch a person arrived in a taxi from Baker Street requesting 20 subscriptions. The request had come from the headquarters of Marks and Spencer. This, more than anything else, helped to convince Michael Young that the project was viable. And, in addition, there was his own personal motivation:

'My main motivation was dislike of advertisements. I disliked them then and I dislike them now. They are mostly lying or near-lying and I though that a body that would give relatively impartial advice to people about the growing amount and variety of goods on the market would actually serve a useful function and be a counterblast to the advertisers.'

The Consumers' Association now operates from very splendid offices near the Embankment close to Charing Cross. But the first tests Michael Young carried out were conducted in their first office, a disused garage in Bethnal Green belonging to University House Settlements and next to Young's office in the Institute of Community Studies.

Funding was obviously a problem, given the lack of institutional support in the 1950s for consumers' interests. As Michael Young explains: 'Labour and capital were locked together and the consumer wasn't represented anywhere on the scene.' If a consumer body was to play some sort of political and lobbying role, it had to seek alternative means of funding. So Young decided to offer a consumer advice service based on a magazine that would provide worthwhile information and service to consumers which they would be willing to pay for. Twenty years later *Which?* magazine has a healthy subscription list of 650,000 and the Association an annual turnover of £16 million.

Funding is crucial for a campaigning lobby group – in the first place to stimulate sufficient publicity to get the group launched and, secondly, to provide an organisation to support its continued existence. Michael Young believes that where the interests of labour or capital are affected, money will be channelled through to promote groups which are sympathetically received by established sectional interests. But what of new social interests, or older ones left out of the funding provided by entrenched interests?

Frank Field was Director of the Child Poverty Action Group for 10 years – from 1969 until he resigned to become MP for Birkenhead. Here he explains how the Quakers played a part in helping to establish the CPAG financially:

'The Child Poverty Action Group was formed in 1965 and, if anybody believes there's not such a thing as political conspiracy in this country, they are wrong.

The political conspiracy is really formed around the Quakers, in that here is a group, some of whom are highly professional and dedicated to bringing about change. The Child Poverty Action Group was formed by them, as was Shelter, and they were behind a number of interesting developments of the social pressure groups of the mid and late 1960s.'

Another source of funding which played a particulalry key role in the 1960s came from the 'Hampstead Worthies' – wealthy liberals who were prepared to encourage and support a number of the new pressure groups that emerged under their influence. One such 'Hampstead Worthy' was Michael Schofield, who began to find the world of 1960 reform groups rather incestuous:

'On various subjects like abortion law reform, cannabis, homosexual law reform, people began to notice that it was the same people signing these petitions or taking part in them. And I was one of them. I think people did tend to say, "Oh him, not him again!" It was a bit worrying, but I was in good company – people like Lord Gardiner, George Melly, Lord Beaumont – so I didn't mind too much.'

Funding for pressure groups is sometimes available from government sources, and in addition many of the constituted groups are similar to charities (Shelter, CPAG and Release, for example) in that their aim is to help certain sectors of the community. But taking money from government sources or setting up as a registered charity is likely to impede the ability of such groups to act overtly in political forums. Michael Schofield explains the problems that Release – set up to help people on drug charges – encountered after receiving a grant from the Home Office.

'Some people were against taking Home Office money; they regarded it as tainted. The National Council for Civil Liberties, for whom I have the greatest respect, will never touch government money. They feel it is going to influence their policy. In fact, I think the Release example is pretty good. They took Home Office money. Then the Home Office got annoyed with them but didn't take the money away. Release learnt a lesson from that. They said, "We will take all the Home Office money we can get, but we'll make sure it's not our only kind of funding'' and therefore they felt free to use that money without becoming dependent on it.

Release was really a street organisation to start with, and was a 'helping' organisation. Like many things that start almost as a charity it gradually turned into a pressure group because those involved found that picking up the pieces wasn't enough ... To the people at Release it was clear that some fairly ordinary young people got arrested for possessing tiny amounts of cannabis, and in those days that meant a prison sentence. It was the business of helping them that made people in Release form the Legalise Cannabis Campaign ... [But such campaigns take] a lot of thinking about. This is one of the things I feel very strongly about pressure groups; we've got a lot of research to do before we are really able to start a campaign. More to the point is that you cannot choose when you are going to start the campaign. Quite often it is some sudden flare-up that starts it and if you are not prepared, then you are caught.'

Being prepared to take advantage of public interest which is often stimulated by media coverage of some event or accident is obviously just part of the ability to use the media. Michael Young:

'You've got to have publicity flair, in that you have got to know about radio, TV and newspapers and what constitutes news and how to give a new twist to something. The pressure groups I've been concerned with have not relied very much on publicity flair, nor on larger-than-life personalities. I'm not one; if I had been maybe I would have thought differently about it. They relied on solid, slogging attention to detail in order to provide a good service to people, so they are going to pay for it and be prepared to back the cause.'

He stresses the need for persistence and the importance of the idea rather than finding a larger-than-life personality who is skilful in grabbing the media's interest:

'I'm sure persistence is absolutely necessary, you've got to decide on something that is right and go for it – over a long period against all opposition. The most important thing of all is a central idea which will appeal to quite a lot of people and which will have all sorts of practical applications and a practical cutting edge to it. If you have got those things and persistence and an organisation, I don't think it matters too much about the larger-than-life personalities.'

Des Wilson, Michael Young and Michael Schofield, who have all made very different contributions to pressure group activity in post-1960 Britain, have in common an identification with liberal-radical politics. Politically opposite, but equally successful in pressure group terms, has been the impact that Mary Whitehouse has had with the National Viewers' and Listeners' Association, of which she is President. There is no doubt that she constitutes a larger-than-life personality who has become extremely adroit at exploiting media coverage. Michael Schofield, who has frequently debated with her, comments:

'I didn't take her too seriously at first, but she has really learnt how to use TV and now she uses it most expertly, and to me that is worrying because charisma with the wrong idea is very dangerous.'

Mary Whitehouse's working environment couldn't be more different from the cramped King's Cross offices of Des Wilson. Her office is in her family home, a large, pretty, pink cottage in rural Essex where she can wander out into the garden in which she takes so much pride. She reminded me of a friendly ageing aunt who seems much more interested in gardening than in manipulating the media for political ends.

In 1963 Mary Whitehouse was a teacher in a large mixed school in the Midlands and one of a group of staff working in the field of sex education. Her anxiety about the content of programmes on the BBC led her to write to the then Director-General, Sir Hugh Greene, and to meet with his deputy, Harman Grisewood. When this did not lead to any improvement from her point of view, she published a manifesto, with her husband Ernest, and the Reverend and Nora Buckland, demanding that the BBC change its policy and restrict the use of violence, bad language and sex in programmes. With little prior experience of such work they printed 2000 petitions and informed the Birmingham

Evening Mail of their 'campaign'. A local reporter came to interview her and asked her if they would be holding a meeting?

> 'I hadn't thought of that actually, but I did a quick think and I said, "Oh yes, we will be holding a public meeting." His next question was, "Will it be in the Birmingham Town Hall?" What I did not know was that Birmingham Town Hall held 2000 people! We did in fact have that meeting, and we knew so little about organising anything like that that all we had was one big poster printed outside the Town Hall.'

Shortly after that story was printed in the Birmingham Evening Mail, nationwide interest was aroused. Letters poured in; the most in one post to her suburban house was 360 letters. Quickly more posters were printed and sent out. Her major anxiety was that very few people would come to Birmingham Town Hall and thus make her campaign a laughing matter.

> 'When the day came I went to school and I tell you all day I was just putting up a little prayer and saying, "Lord, just give us 250, if we get 250 they wouldn't be able to say it was empty." Well ... I walked onto that stage and someone had asked us if they could give us some flowers – we thought they would put some pot plants on the table – and they had put a colossal display of flowers right the way round this apron stage and the place was packed beyond capacity.'

The campaign had a successful launch with national daily newspaper coverage and half a million signatures for their petition. At this point the dilemma of whether to continue as a teacher, or to run the campaign had to be settled. Mary Whitehouse decided to leave teaching and concentrate her energies on the National Viewers' and Listeners' Association (NVALA), which was officially formed in 1965. This permanent pressure group was not set up as a charity in order to allow for maximum political activity. It emerged directly out of the spontaneous success generated by the 'Clean-Up TV Campaign', which she had initiated with her 1963 petition. In 1984 NVALA has one full-time organising secretary and much of its activity depends on decentralised voluntary groups throughout the country. The membership of 30,000 pay only one pound annually for which they receive a copy of the quarterly magazine called *The Viewer and Listener*.

Becoming a political celebrity has its disadvantages in terms of a person's private life, as Mary Whitehouse discovered:

> 'I came under enormous pressure to the extent that threats were sent, so that I was invited to have lunch with the then head of Interpol. I'd no idea why he'd asked me but at the end of the lunch he said to me: "I'm going to give you a telephone number, which I want you to stick on something you take everywhere you go, that will give you a link to me or some of my associates immediately at any time. You must not be in London on your own."

> 'Then came the blasphemy action that I brought against *Gay News* for their poem *Christ*. Well, we had every kind of pressure. We had threats to our lives, we had threats to our property. It was almost unbelievable to see the gays, as they like to be called, marching through London, and they carried two posters, one was the head of Hitler and the other one was the head of me. It was me and Hitler walking side by side through the streets of London.'

The same pressures have been faced by other people in controversial groups. Hilary Jackson of the Abortion Law Reform Association (ALRA) describes the women founders of this association, set up in 1936, as courageous:

> 'They were middle-class women, educated middle-class women, but to talk about such matters as contraception and abortion and women's sexuality was something that just wasn't done. It was something that was kept very quiet indeed, although many thousands, tens and hundreds of thousands of women at the time were being forced into back-street abortions ... Making it a public issue, standing up and saying we want to change this, was something that was very shocking at the time. So by standing up and standing out for what they believed, they created a great scandal, a personal scandal for themselves and they became outcasts of society.'

So far I have concentrated on some of the leading personalities in the world of lobbying because their particular motivation and dedication has helped to shape the face of modern British politics. However, it would be a mistake to think that their success was simply a result of individual personalities. The common denominator of their success is that they identified an idea whose 'time had come', and helped to translate that idea into a social and political movement with the necessary organisation and popular support which made the politicians sit up and listen.

1.2 *Launching a pressure group: Action on Alcohol Abuse*

So how do you go about setting up a lobby group? A list of naïve questions that any aspirant lobby group might pose was drawn up by Mike Daube in a discussion paper written just after he had taken over as Director of ASH (Action on Smoking and Health) in 1973. It is not likely that all or even the majority of these questions could be answered with any degree of certainty. For those who would like more detailed practical advice on campaigning I recommend Des Wilson's book *Pressure: the A to Z of Campaigning in Britain* (1984).

Mike Daube, undoubtedly a successful campaigner, is less well known publicly than the other lobbyists so far discussed. He moved from Shelter to take over ASH from its first Director, John Dunwoody. Subsequently, he helped to launch in 1983 the AAA (Action on Alcohol Abuse). One of the targets for the AAA was the free-spending alcoholic drink industry. Its freedom to promote and advertise alcohol and its vast resources were a major concern for those wishing to tackle the problem of alcoholism in Britain. Of course this was to bring them into conflict with the lobbying capacity of the drinks industry and other industries relying on the sale and distribution of alcohol, ie advertising, packaging and retailing. It is a powerful industry employing 700 000 people who make, distribute and sell alcohol in the UK. There are many large individual companies and of the 27 leading international companies, nine are based in Britain.

Executive Committee Meeting Discussion Paper

ASH. 13.9.1973

What do we want to achieve   i) in the long term?
                           ii) in the short term?

Do we want ASH to be a campaign?
                        Information centre?
                        Fund-raising arm of a research
                        organisation?

Do we want to set any targets for short-term action?

How do we want to use the media?

Do we want to be a 'membership' organisation?

How do we want to be influenced internally?

Do we see ourselves as having primarily a societal function, or medical one, or an educational one?

How important is our charity status?

What are our achievements? How do we want to capitalise on these?

Whom do we want to influence?

Which public/publics are we aiming at?

How do we wish to communicate?

How much access to Government do we have or want?

How much access to media strategies do we have or want?

How much access to party arenas do we have or want?

Do we see ASH as (ideally) growing beyond its present size?

Are there areas where we would step in, had we the resources?

Are we worried about whom we attack and how hard we hit?

Are we prepared to compromise on any major issues - if so, how far?

Can we isolate specific target groups?

(M. Daube 1973)

The drinks industry can rely on many friends in Parliament. Mike Daube estimated that in the 1974–9 Parliament, 74 MPs had direct or indirect financial links with the drinks industry. This is in addition to those MPs who, like David Myles, MP for Banff in the 1979–83 Parliament, had constituency interests concerned with the drinks industry. David Myles had 35 whisky distilling companies in his constituency and therefore felt obliged to act on their behalf as far as he could.

The launch of AAA involved the establishment of a committee with specific aims and a constitution. AAA registered as a limited company and applied for charitable status. These steps are described by Mike Daube in an unpublished document called 'Launching a National Campaign – Action on Alcohol Abuse'. It is revealing to study this article, written 10 years after the discussion paper for ASH in 1973. The AAA launch document is no longer a list of naïve questions but a detailed analysis of their lobby opponents and the type of organisation required to counter-act the drinks industry effectively; most essential was a sponsoring organisation to give the campaign legitimacy. When ASH was started in the early 1970s it was under the auspices of the Royal College of Physicians, following their 1971 report on the harmful effects of smoking. Mike Daube explains what happened with AAA:

> 'We needed, frankly, a sponsoring organisation and a power base. ASH had been established in England and Scotland under the auspices of the Royal College of Physicians' 1971 report on smoking. The equivalent report on alcohol was the 1979 report of the Royal College of Psychiatrists, but it was felt that alcohol was a problem involving so many disciplines that a new organisation could be established under the auspices of more Colleges, perhaps even all.'

Daube feels that getting prestigious supporters from 'interest groups' helps in establishing credibility:

> 'Any organisation backed by the Royal Colleges and their faculties should not want for prestigious supporters. The establishment of AAA has been enthusiastically supported in the *British Medical Journal*, and it may be

assumed that AAA will attract support from many sectors of the medical profession. Most of this support will presumably be relatively inactive, and essentially expressions of goodwill with occasional forays into the public arena, but – as ASH has shown on smoking – little more is needed.'

Relationships with other groups and organisations have to be considered. Even potential allies will not always welcome a new group in the field. They might feel threatened themselves. To avoid this problem Mike Daube and the founders of AAA arranged meetings with representatives of some of the other main organisations in the field. Some welcomed them, but others shied away from co-operation with AAA. And some, in Mike Daube's words, seemed to have 'curious bedfellows'.

> 'I took the minutes of meetings and knew exactly to whom they had been sent. Within a week of both of the first two meetings, held in the House of Commons, copies of the minutes were in the hands of the drinks industry – not from me . . .'

For a successful launching of a new campaign group, it is essential to get the timing right to ensure maximum publicity. Mike Daube felt that for AAA this would be after the 'silly season' but before the major party conferences and the return of Parliament. So the AAA held their press launch on Thursday 15 September at the Royal College of Physicians in London. Mike Daube explains what he did to ensure effective media coverage:

> 'There was obviously much telephoning of media contacts. I sent our first "teaser" press release to get the date in news editors' schedules and the UK Press Gazette Diary, but not giving so much advance information that the story would be blown. Then, three days before the press conference, I sent out a much fuller release with information about the problem, background on AAA, quotable quotes and so on. It's always a gamble: you have to send out some information, but hope the journalists will nonetheless come to the press conference. You also hope that all journalists will observe your embargo (in fact, the *Scotsman* and

Glasgow Herald gave me advance warning that they would break it by a day).'

Forty journalists attended the press conference as well as television and radio crews. The results were worth all the effort – that same day the *Evening Standard* in London ran the headline 'Triple A to Beat the Booze Abuse'. In addition to the coverage in the popular press, the AAA received the endorsement of the prestigious *British Medical Journal*. Mike Daube's assessment of the press launch concludes:

> 'The major disappointment was that we got edged out of the BBC TV 9 O'clock News by an emergency Cabinet meeting. But we made other TV news programmes, almost every radio news and current affairs programme on BBC and commercial radio; and of course there were many additional programmes on following days. Press coverage was better than I had expected. Of the nationals, only the *Daily Mail* for some reason declined to cover us; the qualities gave us excellent play, and the rest were reasonable.'

Not all anti-smoking campaigns are as pre-meditated or as professionally planned as those which Mike Daube worked on. During the 1984 SDP's Annual Conference at Buxton Stuart Holmes, lone lobbyist, took a leaf out of Norman Tebbit's book by riding his bike and poster-trailer to Buxton and staging a one-man protest against smoking outside the main entrance of the conference hall.

1.3 *The post-war expansion of lobbying*

Lobbying is not a new activity. What is new in British politics is the extent to which lobbying has become more public, more organised and more widespread since the Second World War. There have always been interest groups pursuing their professional, business or economic interests. The nineteenth-century railway companies used to provide MPs with seats on the Board of Directors in anticipation of favours. Nowadays, it is not just big business which endeavours to influence government by strategies that have nothing to do with the ballot box. Mike Daube agrees:

'We're attempting to influence behaviour, no question of that. So, of course, are the tobacco and alcohol manufacturers. Between them they spend £300 million a year on advertising and promotion in attempts to change behaviour.'

The period of the 1960s witnessed the flourishing of single-issue pressure groups representing new-found interests, such as those of consumers and the newly educated. Another trend in the 1960s was the politicisation of issues which previously had been categorised as non-political. This was especially noticeable with charities. An explanation of this phenomenon is to be found in three inter-related variables: the governmental process; changing cultural values and attitudes towards politics; and a changing social structure.

Firstly, the impact of governmental process can be understood by a growing disillusionment with the party system and the emergent 'corporatist' state in post-war Britain. The late Robert McKenzie, who taught Politics at the London School of Economics, was more widely known as a TV pundit at election times. His major work, *British Political Parties*, was written in 1955. In that work he made the following point about the relationship between political parties and lobby groups.

'The political parties ... are one of the main channels through which interest groups and both organized and unorganized bodies of opinion can bring their views to the attention of parliamentarians ... Lord Bryce saw American parties as "brokers" whose primary business was to serve various interests and to reconcile them. In the much more homogeneous society of Britain the main parties are inevitably less pre-occupied with this task ...'

But since McKenzie wrote this in 1955 the homogeneity of British society is no longer part of the fixed scenery before which the British political drama is acted out. There is now greater diversity in British society and this diversity is recognised. By the 1960s ethnic, class, regional, religious and age variations had become established as part of a culturally diverse and more pluralistic British society.

The gap between the emergent social interests of the 1950s and '60s, and the inability of the major political parties to represent these new constituent groups within the party framework were two major factors that led to what Dr Geoffrey Alderman and Michael Young identify as an alienation from, or disillusionment with, the political system. Dr Alderman is but one academic who argues that since the Second World War there has been an alienation from the parliamentary system in this country. He says:

'Fewer people turn up to vote at elections and a great many people are disillusioned with the Westminster process. There are a number of reasons for this concerned with the nature of political parties and the public standing of politicians. People do not join political parties today. If they want something done they're much more likely to join a pressure group and through that I think we can discern some failings of the political parties to accommodate the feelings within society, particularly about social and rather sensitive moral issues.'

Michael Young also endorses the view that there has been disillusionment with the conventional political process, especially with the failure, as he sees it, of the radical parties to bring about change.

'Reforming people went at one time into the Liberal or the Labour Parties. If they weren't in a party then they were fairly closely attached to a party. The success of the Labour Government of 1945 in carrying through reforms also showed what the limitations were. Even, in my view, as marvellous a Government as that – certainly ranking with the 1906 Government as a reforming Government – although it did so many good things, it didn't transform society.'

Another crucial change within the governmental process had its roots in the Second World War and led to a phenomenon know as 'corporatism'. In the planning of the war effort, more organisations, particularly those associated with production, were incorporated into the government machinery so as to become part of government. Later, it was not just economic production which benefited from such incorporation; the war-time Government and the post-war

Attlee Government became committed to social reconstruction. This involved a commitment to a Fabian style of
planning, which required drafting in experts. Keynesian
economic philosophy provided a rationale for greater
government intervention for those who may have hesitated
to take part in collective planning justified on socialist or
Fabian grounds. The evils of the centralised 'corporatist'
states associated with Fascism were forgotten. A more
Scandinavian approach was adopted which was committed
to both social and economic engineering. Corporatism
required a degree of consensus amongst the politicians. This
was provided in Britain in the 1950s and '60s by the consensus politics of 'Butskellism'.

Corporatism is a system of interest representation and
elite accommodation. Groups are granted a representational monopoly in exchange for influence over government
policy. With their roots in war-time planning, fed by Fabian
and Keynesian philosophy, and encouraged by a blue sky
which promised an end to both poverty and ideology, the
corporatists 'never had it so good'. There was an extension
of the welfare state and the managed economy, according to
one political writer, Samuel Beer. More and more economic
protectional interest groups were incorporated into government planning. The corporatist age reached its zenith in
1961 with the creation of NEDDY (The National Economic
Development Council) in which the Federation of British
Industries and the Trades Union Congress sat down with
government economic ministers and civil servants to thrash
out broad agreements on economic strategy. This was
during a period of Conservative government. Groups were
encouraged to amalgamate under umbrella organisations
for the sake of greater co-ordination and efficiency of representation. The Confederation of British Industry was set
up in 1965 under a Labour Government with encouragement from George Brown's short-lived Department of
Economic Affairs. Edward Heath's 1970–4 Conservative
Government continued the process and established a
number of quangos under which even more groups were
afforded 'insider' status. The rise of corporatism meant that
conditions were propitious for the proliferation of both
sectional interest groups and promotional organisations.
The message was: 'If you want a voice, then get organised'

and the message was heard not only in the realm of economic policy but also in other arenas, most noticeably that of social policy. The state provided a green light for the emergence of a plethora of lobby groups in the 1960s.

But what is happening now with a Government committed ideologically to rolling back the corporatist state? There are those commentators who argue that the Butskellist consensus, especially on welfare matters, was never deeply rooted and the paraphernalia of government was easy to dismantle. Under the Thatcher Government about 700 quangos have been wound up. But there is a counter-argument, which is particularly relevant to the 'countryside' issues discussed in Chapter 2, that centralisation still continues as planning decisions are taken out of local hands and transferred to the Department of the Environment. Patrick Jenkin, as Secretary of State for the Environment, has also been accused of trampling on local wishes in the much publicised 1984 debate on the abolition of the Metropolitan Authorities, most notably the Greater London Council.

The governmental framework is crucial for understanding the role of lobby groups. The most obvious example is the contrasting part played by lobbyists in Washington compared with Westminster and Whitehall. However, the governmental framework does not operate in a cultural vacuum, hence the need to look more broadly at the changing values and attitudes in post-war Britain.

Andrew Roth, an American political journalist who came to live in Britain in the early 1950s, has formed his own company, Parliamentary Profiles. He observes this about the deferential and establishment-guided attitudes towards politics prevalent in Britain in the 1950s:

'Of the changes in all aspects of British society since I first arrived here in 1950 the greatest has been the opening out of British society. In the early days one was very much struck by how up-tight various institutions were, including the press. Pressmen, political correspondents like myself, for example, would know a great deal more than they would report because they didn't think it was "nice" to report about certain things. They felt themselves almost part of the establishment and of course the senior politicians took

advantage of this. They would confide things privately to them with the assurance it would not appear
in the newspaper. Now that's changed very con-
siderably, thanks to a number of institutions like *Private Eye* and the breakout of the BBC in *That Was The
Week That Was*. In the 1960s came the great
breakthrough; the Profumo case helped. I was some-
what involved in that because I was the first one to
write about that openly, although there were a
number of Fleet Street papers which knew about the
Profumo case but kept their mouths shut, or their
presses quiet. That sort of thing began the great
breakout, the great transformation of British politics
. . .'

The 1960s was also a period of great optimism, when
people began to shake off deferential attitudes and began to
seek alternative political solutions. As Des Wilson puts it:

'It was a time when it seemed possible to try anything
and do anything. It was a marvellous decade and I
only wish such a decade could return. A lot of younger
people were coming into all sorts of activity; unaware
of the rules and normal ways of doing things and
"doing their own thing". You could say it was the
arrival on the scene of the newly educated class of this
country; the product of all the changes that had taken
place since the Second World War.'

Hilary Jackson feels that the new mood of the 1960s
generated a mood of impatience with ALRA's lack
of success. The Association was effectively refounded
with a new determined type of women campaigner in
charge. She comments:

'I think there was an atmosphere within the '60s. I
don't think it was just a myth that the social atmosphere changed, that there was a desire for more liberal
reform ... People actually had the courage and the
honesty to speak about it in public. People weren't
going to be blinkered, they weren't going to be dishonest and that was part of that freedom that came
alive ... By the early '60s ALRA was taken over by a
group of women who had become impatient that
nothing had happened.'

The election of a Labour Government in 1964, after 13 years of Conservative administrations, was seen by some as a new radical dawn. This victory contributed to the optimistic mood. Frank Field was a young Labour supporter at that time who subsequently became disillusioned with the Government:

'I can remember those election results coming in and believing we now had elected a radical Government that was going to, as previous radical Governments had done in our history, make one of those big changes in the way we ran our society. But the campaign on poverty ran into the sands of official committees and the Government was not able to deliver. I think much of the bitterness and nastiness and hatred, which is engendered now in our political system, comes from the fact we are still waiting for that big sea-change that was never delivered in 1964 and has not been delivered since. The system has gone sour.'

But before it went sour the mood of the times began challenging the conventional and established way of life. The post-war cultural consensus based on deference was cracking-up. With it came the view that everything was possible and everything was political. Politics began to penetrate into all aspects of life and everything seemed capable of political relevance. Even language and hairstyles assumed a political significance. Apart from the catalyst provided by corporatism, another cause of the heightened political consciousness of the period was the disillusionment with the consensus politics of the 1950s. Instead of expected affluence, poverty was 'rediscovered' in the 1960s. The acclaimed 'end of ideology' turned out to be hollow.

There is no doubting the mood of this 'pluralist age' in the second half of the 1960s. In the *Directory of Pressure Groups and Representative Associations* (Shipley, 1979), over half the groups listed were formed *after* 1960. But it was not only politically specific groups like Shelter and CPAG that were mushrooming. Out of the political darkness voluntary associations joined the political mêlée; a decade earlier this would have led to mass resignations amongst their memberships. Charities were prepared to risk their tax-exempt status in order to join the fray. Middle-class unions began

to use the militant rhetoric of their working-class counter-
parts. Even the law was dragged into the arena. For the first
time a whole generation, whether as squatters, tenants, wel-
fare-dependents or women, started to use the law, not only to
protect but also to demand their rights. The era of a deferential and passive citizenry was passing. The institu-
tionalisation of politics into ritualised conflicts between the
parties was over. Lobby groups stole political initiative from
the slow-moving and moribund party structure. It was not
just the Labour Party which seemed like an old stage coach –
as Harold Wilson once described it – in the age of jet travel.

Political penetration into walks of life previously
regarded as non-political could be seen in a number of areas.
Des Wilson describes how it happened in Shelter's case:

> 'Shelter was the first charity that could really involve
> itself heavily and openly in politics and it's always
> been assumed this was a carefully made and conscious
> decision. The fact of the matter was I didn't know what
> the charity laws were. It was only after Shelter had
> been going several months that it was drawn to my
> attention that it wasn't the done thing for a charity.'

Tension between political activity and charitable status
continues. In a report published in 1984, the National
Council for Voluntary Organisations urged the Charity
Commission to revise their guidelines to allow charities
'freedom to engage in advocacy'. The report argues that
charities should be free to make a case for and against legislative reforms. Nicholas Hinton, the Director of NCVO,
argued in a letter to *The Times* (12 May, 1984) that the
confusion at present is based on the interpretation of the
term 'political activity' which charities are not supposed to
engage in. He suggested that the term 'political activity' in
relationship to charities be more normally restricted to 'only
activities whose aims include ... the influencing of the
electoral process in favour of (or against) any person or
party'. This would allow charities to engage in debates on
public policy – as many, like Christian Aid or War on Want,
already do – without fear of losing the tax-exemption that
accompanies charitable status. If this were achieved, then
charities could operate more openly as lobbying
organisations.

Underlying these developments in the governmental process and public attitudes in the 1960s were a number of changing elements in the structure of British society. More immigrants introduced different values; better-educated citizens encouraged changing beliefs about society; changing occupational opportunities broke up old communities; television arrived; living standards were achieved which would have been unrealisable before the Second World War. These elements provided the social fluidity which enabled the mobilisation of new social interests such as those of consumers and environmentalists.

Michael Young, who, as well as being a social reformer, is a prominent sociologist, suggests that the emergence of lobby groups in the 1960s resulted from disillusionment with the conventional political system and the coming of television. In addition, he cites a third factor:

> 'Another factor is the extension of education, including higher education, producing more people with more ideas about what should be done in the way of improvement in society in this country and on a world scale. There are a lot of loose supporters for good causes that have been produced by education. Society has become more fluid, the political parties have less of a strangle-hold, there are more initiatives which can now flower.'

Allowing initiative to flower, however, is not without its political consequences. A political process which encourages more demands will have the difficulty of reconciling them. Greater political mobilisation and more articulated interests create the problem of interest aggregation for the policy makers. 'Let a hundred flowers bloom' may be the message but, unlike flowers, the members of a politicised society are not content to be overlooked by the gardener. Des Wilson illustrates this point:

> 'I always remember Jim Callaghan after he retired as Prime Minister. I met him at a function and we talked about pressure groups, and he said, "You're making the country more difficult to govern", and I said, "The country should be difficult to govern because a country that is easy to govern is easy to misgovern, it's easy to dictate to, it's easy to oppress". A democracy should be

vibrant, there should be constant challenges to decisions in the way things are done.'

1.4 *Benefits for democracy*

Lobby groups provide an alternative form of participation in the political system to the more traditional means of joining a party. This is true even if, as Conservative MP Julian Critchley argues, the British are not so politically involved as citizens of other nations, such as the Americans.

> 'The overwhelming majority of the British are not interested in working in politics; it's not an activity that stimulates the British as a whole. I think you would find in the United States, because of their racial composition, their ethnic groups and their huge geography and a much larger middle-class (which is more articulate), that the Congressman rather than the Member of Parliament is subject all the time to a series of pressures of single-issue groups, and their life is far more hectic than mine.'

This reluctance to engage in politics might explain why the British are more likely to set up a pressure group than join a political party. Julian Critchley continues:

> 'In a sense it's due to the failure of the political parties themselves. Less than one per cent of the population are prepared to join a political party of their choice and spend Thursday nights of the week on political activity. This means that the other 99 per cent, when something happens that energises them, interests them particularly, instead of marching along to the political party locally, they form their own groupings. So that the anti-abortion lobby has nothing to do with the Conservative Party or Labour Party. It stands on its own.'

Hence, pressure groups provide a means for the ordinary citizen to have a voice in public affairs without having to undertake the commitment of joining a political party.

Also, through participation in a single-issue campaign

ordinary persons might come to understand the political system better, and through the support of fellow campaigners might be encouraged to take part in a way they never previously thought possible. This activity can promote a sense of personal political efficacy.

The abortion issue encouraged a large number of women to take part in political lobbying. The opportunity was provided by the Abortion Act of 1967 and the subsequent attempts through private Members' bills to challenge and amend it. A series of attacks on the Abortion Act were posed by James White MP in 1975, William Benyon MP in 1977 and John Corrie MP in 1979. This reflected the parliamentary manifestation of a much broader mobilisation of opinion and activity throughout the country. New groups were formed. On the side of the 1967 Abortion Act was the new 'umbrella' organisation, the National Abortion Campaign, formed in 1975. At its first conference in October of that year it revealed its radical nature by adopting the feminist slogan 'Abortion on demand – a woman's right to choose'. In 1976 The Co-ordinating Committee in Defence of the 1967 Abortion Act was formed. Challenging the abortion legislation were the Society for the Protection of the Unborn Child (SPUC), which had been formed in 1967, Life in 1970, and the National Pro-Life Committee in 1974.

Many women who would have regarded themselves as non-political were to be swept up by the moral and political issues associated with abortion. Women took to the streets in large numbers; demonstrators packed Trafalgar Square and lobbyists swamped Parliament. During the lobbying of 1975, prompted by James White's bill, Hilary Jackson of ALRA met a woman who had travelled down from Prime Minister Harold Wilson's constituency in Liverpool.

The woman felt angry about the proposed restrictions on abortion in James White's Bill, but, although she wanted to do something about it, she did not feel able to lobby Harold Wilson himself because of his eminent position. Encouraged by the stewards, she eventually put in a green card requesting to see her MP. On discovering that he was not in the House of Commons she was then persuaded by the stewards to telephone him at 10 Downing Street. Her telephone call was taken by his secretary who made a note of her views, apologised to her for the Prime Minister's absence and thanked her for taking the trouble to contact him. Hilary Jackson (ALRA):

> 'And that lady, she hadn't met Harold Wilson, she hadn't met the Prime Minister, but she'd actually become less powerless, she had been convinced she could do things, she could try to further her point of view. I think she would go away and do it again, so that whole experience was something that was valuable for her and I think for all the women that then were involved. .... People came to lobby who never thought it was possible before, they thought it wasn't their job to do things like that and they wouldn't have thought they could have any influence.'

For those who do want a more active and full-time role in politics, pressure groups and interest groups allow for a career in politics outside the normal route through membership of a political party into Parliament. The new industry of pressure group politics has provided a new career structure.

These two careers are not mutually exclusive. Frank Field moved from pressure group to Parliament in 1979. David Myles' involvement with an interest group – the National Farmers' Union – led to his parliamentary career as a Conservative MP. A more senior NFU member, Sir Henry Plumb – former President of the NFU, was elected in 1979 to the European Parliament as a Conservative member, as was Sir Frederick Catherwood – previously Director of the CBI. Mike Daube, after he had become established as the prominent Director of ASH, was invited by two political parties to stand as a parliamentary candidate. Many Labour MPs worked previously for the trade unions that sponsored them.

So much for individuals either as ordinary participants or career politicians. But what advantages does lobbying bring to the democratic system? Do lobby organisations distort or enhance the democratic process? In subsequent chapters I shall look at some of the criticisms of pressure group politics, but here are the major advantages which I believe lobby groups provide under the British parliamentary system of government.

1   *Political Monitoring*: monitoring the activities, decisions and utterances of the Government, the administration and politicians.

2 *Informing*: providing information on issues for the Government, administrations and politicians.

3 *Protecting Minorities*: representing minority groups, interests and ideologies which might be ignored by the broad coalitions which make up the main political parties.

4 *Sustaining Debate*: maintaining discussion on issues which the press and Parliament might have otherwise ignored.

5 *Mobilising*: providing citizens with an alternative form of political participation in a campaign which can generate a greater sense of personal political efficacy than is usual in the bureaucratically organised mass parties.

6 *Countervailing*: providing at least some means of counteracting the activities of powerful groups and interests which might otherwise achieve influence through lack of opposition.

Des Wilson believes that the real opposition to government and powerful interests is not to be found in Her Majesty's Official Opposition in Parliament but in the pressure groups outside.

2 Pressure in the country

Britain is too small a country with too large a population for the debate about the use of the countryside to be a matter for farmers alone. The lobbying and counter-lobbying between agricultural, environmental, animal protection and leisure interests means that 'use of the countryside' is an issue with a high profile in British politics and is not without controversy. Lobbying activity on the use of the British countryside and its resulting paperwork has caused more tree-felling than Dutch elm disease ever did.

In recent years the influential position of farmers represented by the NFU (National Farmers' Union) has come under attack. This is partly to do with a number of farming practices which have become the focus of widespread criticism, such as straw burning and pesticide use. Crop spraying and straw burning have led to incidents which provided evidence that farmers are not only a threat to British wildlife, in that they poison or destroy their hedgerow habitat, but are also proving a threat to human beings. Deaths in car accidents were caused by smoke from straw burning; farm workers were found to be inadequately trained and to have little understanding of the effects on the food chain and water supply of the chemicals used on the land.

But the attack has mainly been provoked for another reason: the huge changes wrought on the face of rural Britain by new farming practices. The loss of 140,000 miles of hedgerow since the Second World War, the loss of 185,000 acres of moorland, and the loss of 80 per cent of natural chalkland downs to crop growing might speak highly of the greater economic efficiency of British farming and the grants system provided by the Ministry of Agriculture, Forestry and Fisheries which stimulated those changes. But to the conservationist these losses are just another example of short-term thinking which would have long-term consequences for the countryside.

The 1981 Wildlife and Countryside Act was an attempt to counteract these consequences, but it did little to appease conservationists and actually provoked further resentment of landowners since they were the ones who gained from the Act's provision. As a result of this Act landowners are handsomely compensated for not ploughing up fields, chopping down trees or draining marshes. It now encourages existing owners, or business interests to buy sites of special scientific interest (sssi) and threaten to plough them or plant soft wood trees for cash crops. The tax payer is the loser when huge amounts are then paid out in compensation. All this is happening at a time when farming is seen to be one of the most lucrative areas of business, benefiting from rate exemption domestically and huge grants through the eec's common agricultural policy.

To the picture painted by environmentalists and conservationists of the 'rape' of the British countryside can be added the trans-European spectre of wasteful butter mountains and wine lakes, and winding lines of boycotted lorries, victims of the lamb war. To this scene of rural conflict should be added the lobby interests of the taxpayers and consumers who are subsidising this state of affairs.

In addition to the issues of agriculture versus conservation and eec food policies there is the controversy over leisure pursuits. What sports should be permitted? How easily reconciled are they with agricultural activities? New leisure industries are taking an interest in the British countryside. Old leisure interests continue their carnage as hunters lock horns with the anti-hunting groups. Pursuing its gentle efforts to allow public access to common land is one of the oldest rural lobby groups of all, the Common Open Spaces and Footpaths Preservation Society, founded in 1865. A hundred years later, and very non-Victorian in style, are the Friends of the Earth. Inspired by the American Friends of the Earth, a British organisation was established in 1970.

2.1   *The evolution of countryside lobby groups*

In Chapter 1 I looked at developments in lobbying in British politics since the 1950s. A longer and more specific analysis of the developments of the environmental movement is to be found in the study, *Environmental Groups in Politics* (1983) written by Philip Lowe and Jane Goyder. In their survey of 77 pressure groups they chose to make a basic distinction between *interest* and *principle* groups. Interest groups were defined as those based on unions or the major groups that represent professional bodies or business, or some other interest which identifies the membership. Principle groups are those which have in common a set of values. The test distinguishing these two categories is whether one can automatically identify who the potential membership would be. With an interest group like the National Union of Teachers or the Royal College of Surgeons the membership is self-defining. But with the Friends of the Earth or the League against Cruel Sports there is no way of knowing from whom the group's support will come. What the members have in common is a shared set of values and attitudes, and a common orientation to a specific issue.

Lowe and Goyder then subdivided principle groups into two categories of *emphasis* and *promotional*, depending on whether they are concerned with defending or challenging existing values and power relations. Friends of the Earth and Greenpeace, being more radical groups, would be classified as promotional, whilst the National Trust and the Council for the Protection of Rural England are emphasis groups.

Lowe and Goyder describe the development of the environmental movement as uneven and episodic. They identify three eras when environmental organisations expanded or new groups were formed. Firstly, 1896 to 1905, when groups like the Selborne Society, the Royal Society for the Protection of Birds, the Coal Smoke Abatement Society and the National Trust were founded. Secondly, the inter-war years, when groups such as the League Against Cruel Sports (1924), the Council for the Protection of Rural England (1926), the Ramblers' Association (1935) and the Youth Hostel Association (1930) were formed. The third era emerged in the late 1950s and continued through to the mid '70s with new organisations like the Civic Trust (1957), Friends of the Earth (1970) and Greenpeace (1972).

Lowe and Goyder explain this uneven development in terms of the impact of periods of sustained economic expansion:

'We would suggest that environmental groups arose at those times as more and more people turned to count the mounting external costs of unbridled economic growth and sought to re-assert non-material values.'

The underlying economic expansion was to generate doubts about the life-style that was being created:

'Environmental groups gave expression to doubts about industrialisation, particularly in relation to its impact on urban life and urban growth. . . . Common to all environmental groups of the 1890s period was a moral and aesthetic revulsion to the contemporary city.'

As well as displaying hostility to the destruction of human values as economic growth swept away older, less efficient, traditions of community life, the environmental groups began to demand an end to 'rampant individualism' and its anti-social consequences. 'Two other values which late Victorian environmentalism derived from the wider intellectual reaction of economic liberalism were its collectivism and its rejection of *laissez-faire*' (Lowe and Goyder 1983). The view was that the State was justified in constraining individual behaviour especially in the case of a factory polluting a river, a landowner enclosing land, or a sportsman shooting rare birds.

The extension of the State's role was to reach a new peak in the 1945 to 1951 Labour Government of Clement Attlee and its new system of planning controls. This system gave the impetus for the formation of local protection groups that would lobby local authorities about the use of their newly granted planning power.

A criticism of the argument put forward by Lowe and Goyder is that the 1920s could hardly be considered a period of economic growth so intense that it provided the stimulus for an anti-economic growth outlook which then generated demands for greater collectivist control of economic activity. When I put this criticism to Philip Lowe, he pointed out that this was a 'fairly crude' initial model:

'. . . at the end of the day what matters is the impact of economic growth on certain social groups and certain regions and clearly there were parts of Britain in the late 1920s [and] throughout most of the early 1930s that were booming economically, particularly parts of southern Britain. It was a great period for the expansion of the motor car industry, for example. So some people were able to experience the fruits of economic growth and also the problems of it. You can see that in the south of Britain with the enormous spread of London; this caused people great alarm, particularly those living in the Home Counties. It encouraged them to organise, so as to restrict the spread of London and the impact of the motor car. I think the impact of the business cycle is clearest in the late 1960s with the appearance of environmental groups that were specifically set up to challenge economic growth. This was true certainly of the early Friends of the Earth and a whole range of other groups which saw economic growth as the major cause of environmental problems.'

A second criticism of Lowe and Goyder's thesis is that the cultural and ideological response from the anti-business ethos of the environmental lobby might be more readily identified with promotional groups, which by definition are radical, rather than with emphasis groups, some of which, although accepting the need for state intervention, would not accept the anti-profit and anti-business ideology. Philip Lowe:

'Inherent in environmentalism and environmental values is a reaction to unregulated economic activity, and to that whole set of values associated with nineteenth-century *laissez-faire* economics. In other words it is a rejection of simple market forces and of notions of private profit and private property.'

A third criticism arises out of their theory that environmental groups emerge from the problems associated with periods of rapid economic activity and high points in the business cycle, and so environmental lobbying will decline during periods of reduced economic activity, such as the 1970s and '80s in Britain. Philip Lowe asserts:

'One of the things we saw, certainly since the late '70s, is that some of those big projects that were the cutting edge of growth, the third London airport, the Channel tunnel and the massive programme of nuclear expansion for energy, have all been curtailed or postponed and that this in a way robs environmental groups of what is the stuff of their activity ... and therefore one sees a certain lull in environmental politics.'

Yet critics observe that what evidence there is would seem to point to no such lull in the activities of the environmental pressure groups in the 1980s. Government policies on the green belt, planning practice, EEC policies on farming subsidies and the big issues like nuclear power continue to provide a target for environmentalists. Perhaps it is that environmental groups have 'come of age' and, like consumers, have to be taken into account rather than dismissed as peripheral to real politics. The 'Greens' are now an established part of the political scene in western Europe and America.

2.2 *Organisational styles*

There is no one model for organisational efficiency for environmental lobby organisations. Not unexpectedly, interest groups like the NFU, based on wealthy economic interests such as farming, will have a permanent and centralised bureaucracy, as well as a network of local representatives. Pressure groups are more likely to vary in style depending on wealth, objectives and strategy. Those groups which formed in the Victorian era are more likely to have developed a more elitist style of organisation. The post-1960s promotional pressure groups are more likely to attempt to build up local groups, encourage wider participation and try to generate a broader social base for their cause. But not exclusively so, for some promotional groups argue that they are more efficient with just a small staff of full-time workers and a centralised organisation. Mike Daube describes just such a model in an article in *Marketing* (Oct 1979).

'The most effective pressure groups tend to be those which are run by a small, highly professional core: members can be useful (not least in paying subscriptions) but they can also be a hindrance and often fail to realise that time spent servicing them could have been spent more profitably.'

A small, professional organisation might be more efficient, but it can also generate problems.

The relationship between how groups organise themselves internally and their involvement with the external political world is one of the points raised in Lowe and Goyder's book. This is not just of academic interest because groups need to present a certain face to the outside world and they have got to sort out their own internal domestic concerns before they can do that. Philip Lowe explains this point further:

> 'You often find internal conflicts within any pressure group, but those conflicts have to be managed because a group has to present a united front to the outside world. This unity for a pressure group is a weakness and so groups spend a lot of their time managing their own internal affairs.'

Another way in which external political structures influence the shape of internal organisational structures is that caused by centralised government and centralised media. These institutions find it easier to work with groups that have a clear hierarchy of responsibility and a recognised public spokesman. This allows a civil servant or journalist to obtain an authoritative statement about a group's attitude or policy stance with relative ease and with the certainty of knowing it is not likely to be contradicted or denied by other factions within the group. Thus lobby groups are more likely to be London-based with ease of access to Whitehall and Fleet Street. This can lead to resentments amongst the provincial ordinary members who may feel they are being ignored whilst the leadership are seen on television hob-nobbing with the mighty and powerful in London. This is more likely to be the case of radical promotional groups, where often leadership is distrusted or disliked in principle. This can produce tension between leaders and members, particularly if members feel excluded from key decisions. No such tension seems to afflict the Georgian Society, however; the Secretary who replied to Lowe and Goyder's questionnaire stated: 'We are a most undemocratic body . . . controlled by a self-perpetrating oligarchy.' Such emphasis groups tend to have a closer relationship with government bodies and are subsequently less willing to rock the boat than the more radical promotional groups.

More democratically oriented are the 1960s pressure groups. 'Democracy' and 'Participation' were two highly favoured slogans of the '60s generation who inspired and joined the new lobby groups of that era, and the alternative culture was stressed by those groups.

Friends of the Earth was one of the radical promotional groups established in the 1960s tradition of the alternative culture. Their very objectives as a group were counter-cultural. They stressed smallness, concern for the environment and a better life – if only economic institutions could be made less wieldly, less bureaucratic, less profit-centred and less concerned with short-term market goals. They propounded a philosophy that would be the key to a more practical way of life.

FOE is organised on two levels. The first involves 300 local groups who develop their own initiatives on practical environmental projects in their locality. The second level is the national organisation with 25 000 members who tend to pay subscriptions but are otherwise passive. The national organisation is based in Islington with 18 full-time staff. Their main aim is to influence central decision-making, whether of the Government or the larger manufacturing companies which are also likely to be based in London.

This centralised lobbying frequently involves the production of documents on some environmental topic, such as the use of pesticides or alternative energy sources, which contain great technical detail and require the co-operation of sympathetic supporters who have expertise in such matters. Charles Secrett, a full-time co-ordinator at their Islington office sees FOE's role as providing an 'intellectual cattle-prod' to encourage government action by a combination of argument and publicity.

One of their most publicised campaigns was to 'Save the Whale'. They were able to lobby at three levels: firstly, by organising mass rallies with thousands crowding Trafalgar Square in 1979; secondly, by approaching certain individual companies in Britain which used whale meat (typically pet food companies) and whale oil (mainly the leather industry), and suggesting economically viable substitutes; and thirdly, by producing well documented research dossiers on the distribution of whales and the effect of continued whaling on world stocks. These were presented to the British Government and the International Whaling Commission which seeks to establish a voluntary system of quotas for the whaling industry.

Very often the Government will not act until the public has been mobilised and a degree of support for a campaign is discernible. For this reason some groups endeavour to build up public sympathy for their campaign whilst not bothering too much with the size of their membership. The League Against Cruel Sports, together with other animal groups, paid NOP Market Research Ltd to conduct a public opinion poll, published in 1983 and entitled *Animal Issues and their Influence on Voting*. It was a sample of 2135 electors, and was used to publicise animal issues in the run-up to the 1983 General Election. It showed that fox-hunting was disapproved of by 65 per cent of the sample, deer-hunting by 81 per cent, and a similar proportion disapproved of hare-coursing.

Organising a mass rally or a mass petition is another way of showing the degree of support for an issue. Lobby groups at relevant times will draw a distinction between the size of their membership and their public sympathisers.

Currently the Council for the Protection of Rural England (CPRE), founded in 1926, is concerned with the size and composition of its membership. It is undertaking, according to its 1983 Annual Report, 'an ambitious recruitment programme'. CPRE in 1984 has 30 000 members, mainly in the shire counties. This membership is upper middle-class, and wealthy and prestigious, but also ageing and dwindling. CPRE has a central office in London with 15 full-time staff. Robin Grove-White, its director, says:

> 'Our membership is a different constituency from bodies like Friends of the Earth or Greenpeace. We are, if you like, more establishment and that is a reflection of our history, because we were set up more than 50 years ago in the 1920s ... Things were very different in those days. There was a much greater harmony between agriculture and other amenity or environmental issues then, and our membership reflects that still. So in the 1980s with a new range of issues we are trying to extend our membership now and reach a new range of people as well.'

The membership drive was made possible by a grant from the Countryside Commission. Clearly CPRE is worried about its elitist image based on the landed gentry of the shire counties. Perhaps it is on the point of shifting from an emphasis to a promotional group status. Part of this would explain why it is actively seeking a broader social base by recruiting from urban areas in the hope of attracting a wider class membership.

Richard Course of the League Against Cruel Sports also sees a shift in class background in the membership of animal welfare groups:

> 'The animal welfare movement as a whole was very much a middle-class thing in the '40s, '50s and '60s. In the '70s ordinary people, that is a mixture of people, became involved as well.'

The class nature of environmental and conservationist groups has been a disputed part of the public imagery of these groups ever since Anthony Crosland declared that environmentalism is an overwhelmingly middle-class concern. Crosland, having been the Secretary of State for the Environment between 1974 and 1976 in the Labour Government, wrote this about the conservationist lobby:

> 'Their approach is hostile to growth and indifferent to the needs of ordinary people. It has a manifest class bias and reflects a set of middle and upper-class value judgements.'

In their book *Environmental Groups in Politics* Lowe and Goyder examined this notion of the relationship between class and environmental policies. Firstly, they found that the membership of environmental groups was indeed predominantly middle-class, although some groups, like the Royal Society for the Protection of Birds, had appeal to a lower middle-class membership, whilst angling clubs had a mainly working-class membership. But the leadership of environmental groups was overwhelmingly middle class. Secondly, they found that there was some evidence from surveys and public opinion polls to show that, although the working class were less likely to join a group, they nevertheless cared about environmental and conservation issues, especially about pollution and health. Environmental *interest* was not just a middle-class phenomenon.

Conservation and environmental organisers and representatives (as in most British institutions apart from trade unions) are admittedly not often working-class. But to deduce from this, as Crosland apparently did, that working-class people are not concerned with the environment is wrong. The environment, like war and peace, is not simply a narrow question of class interest, although on some issues, like the opposition to new housing estates or new industrial zones, it is not uncommon for middle-class communities to be more vocal, organised and adamant in order that their life-style should not be affected.

Single-issue pressure groups are not always concerned with the promotion of radical causes. Some of the most effective lobbyists have been local, spontaneous pressure groups in otherwise conservative communities when local interests are at stake. The village of Hook is a good example of this and I shall return to it in a later section of this chapter.

Another crucial dynamic element in the organisation of lobby groups is their relationship with other groups – forming alliances on an issue, or even setting up a permanent co-ordinating organisation for a concentrated long-term lobby campaign.

In Chapter 1 I quoted Mike Daube's explanation of how useful it could be for a pressure group to show it has the support of respectable interest groups. ASH, for example, had the Royal College of Physicians as its sponsoring organisation. This support can provide both instant legitimacy and greater access to decision-makers. Here Hilary Jackson (ALRA) explains the advantage to the abortion movement of having the support of the medical establishment even though it was initially opposed to the abortion reform provisions introduced in 1967:

> '... since then there has been a radical change in the opinions and support of organisations such as the British Medical Association and Royal College of Obstetricians and Gynaecologists. Certainly at the time of John Corrie's Bill they were a great source of support, actually saying that the rights established by the 1967 Act should not be taken away.'

Environmental and conservation groups will often seek the co-operation of academics and experts on issues like nuclear fuel, soil erosion, natural habitat destruction and its ecological impact, or the harmful effects of lead in petrol. This co-operation ensures that they are armed with relevant, factual information, but equally important it adds a scientific legitimacy to their campaigns.

Whether the issue is lead in petrol, abortion, or action on smoking, lobby groups rarely act alone. It is important to understand the way in which they work together in the political system as an environmental lobby. A few – the CPRE, the Civic Trust, the Council for Environmental Conservation, FOE, the National Trust and the RSPB – enjoy contacts with the majority of environmental groups. 'They are the effective focal points of the environmental movement,' according to Lowe and Goyder.

Amongst the animal protection groups, it was the League Against Cruel Sports which played a leading part in setting up an umbrella organisation called the Animal Protection Alliance in 1982; other member groups include the National Anti-vivisection Society, Compassion in World Farming, Animal Aid and the British Union for the Abolition of Vivisection.

Co-operating with other groups, as the League Against Cruel Sports realises, involves not only sharing a common objective, but also compatibility in tactics. Of foremost consideration is the question of direct action and the extent to which a lobby group considers it effective to act illegally in pursuit of agreed goals. The Hunt Saboteurs' Association (formed by a splinter group within LACS in 1963) and the Animal Liberation Front can prove an embarrassment to those animal rights groups seeking long-term changes in the law, which might be put in jeopardy if they are seen to act irresponsibly by supporting 'immediate' action which goes beyond the law. Examples of such action include illegally breaking into vivisection laboratories and freeing animals or daubing the houses of animal experimenters with paint; and in 1984 animal rights protesters put bleach into Sunsilk hair shampoo on sale in Boots, the chemists, to protest about the use of animals in testing new cosmetic products. The Animal Liberation Front claimed responsibility for this.

Another example of 'immediate' action took place in 1979 when the International Whaling Commission met in

London. 'Blood' (actually red vegetable dye) was thrown over the Japanese delegation in protest at the fact that Japan, along with Russia, still operated a large-scale whaling industry. This incident did bring international publicity to the issue but it also split the environmental groups. Charles Secrett of FOE explains the worry he had at the time about this action:

> 'It was an aggressive act, it was a muted act of violence and in a sense it could have also escalated into other more aggressive acts. At the same time we saw that people were wandering around defacing Japanese cars and the Japanese were identified in the minds of the most fanatical conservationists and animal protectionists as somehow being solely responsible for the destruction of these magnificent creatures. Now that sort of xenophobia is a dangerous thing and I think that as far as Friends of the Earth is concerned, and all the other radical groups, it is not legitimate to use violence.'

Friends of the Earth were more certain, however, about the direct action taken at an ancient woodland and chalk grassland wildlife site at Mollards Wood near Biggin Hill (Greater London) in May 1984. The landowner was clearing an area which was the habitat of some very rare orchids and butterfly species. FOE supporters chained themselves across paths to prevent bulldozers gaining access to the land and also surrounded the bulldozers. Eventually, because they were unable to maintain a physical presence on the site permanently, the bulldozers finally went in and cleared half the ancient woodland. This story shows that FOE is willing to engage in at least some for of direct action. Not so the Council for the Protection of Rural England. CPRE has a very respectable and law-abiding style which is embodied in its constitution and enshrined in this declaration: 'To take any other *lawful* action to promote the aforesaid objects [of the CPRE]'.

Although LACS also distances itself from the more aggressive animal protection groups it is not above dirty tricks. They have used 'moles' to infiltrate hunts, for example. Mike Huskisson's *Outfoxed*, published in 1983, contains photographs taken by someone posing as a member of the hunt in order to illustrate the League's claims about the horrors of hunting. Ironically, a counter-mole, Michael O'Reilly, recently worked for LACS whilst at the same time providing inside information for the hunting community.

It is actually the farmer not the environmentalist who has the best chance of succeeding with direct-action tactics. To protect a wild wetland site at Halvergate Marshes on the Norfolk Broads, conservationists chained themselves to a bulldozer and mechanical digger to prevent 90 acres of land being ploughed up. The landowner, David Wright, had just had a compensation offer of £22 250 under the 1981 Wildlife and Countryside Act withdrawn on grounds of cost. David Wright's direct action, well within the law, was to spray the grass with herbicide and thus, in one fell swoop, destroy the grass and the direct-action efforts of the conservationists.

2.3 *Three views of British democracy: corporatist, pluralist and Burkean*

The style and strategies of lobby groups are influenced by a number of internal organisational factors which were discussed in the preceding section of this chapter, using environmental groups as illustrations. One *external* factor which helps to determine the strategy of a lobby organisation is its corporate perception of how the political system works. The British system of government is one described constitutionally as parliamentary government. But it would be naïve to think that Parliament is the centre of effective political power. Power is not easily located in a complex, industrial democracy with its system of parliamentary elections and prime ministerial government. But throughout the research for the BBC TV series and this book, those who were prepared to accept that lobbying can and does influence government policy held one of three views of British democracy: corporatist, pluralist and Burkean.

Corporatism and the incorporation of agricultural interests into the machinery of government decision-making
Corporatism has already been looked at in Chapter 1. The

term refers to a highly centralised form of government in which sectional interests are incorporated into the process of policy-formulation and decision-making. Corporatism provided one of the stimuli for the emergence of sectional interest groups in post-war Britain. Representatives of sectional interests were invited to join government bodies, consultative committees and quangos and thus gained direct access to government departments. In his article 'Parties, Pressure Groups and the British Political Press' (*Pressure Groups in Britain*, Kimber and Richardson, 1974), Robert McKenzie wrote:

> 'In no other country are the sectional interests ... brought more intimately into consultation in the process of decision-making in government and political parties.'

Incorporating lobby groups into the process of formulating public policy and also in implementing it (the Law Society, for example, runs the Legal Aid scheme), has two advantages for government. Firstly, it results in the provision of a wider set of data because the differing and sometimes competing interests furnish a wealth of technical detail not easily available to government departments. Secondly, it helps to legitimate public policy: by taking part in the formulation of policy, groups, their leaders and members are less likely to criticise and reject governmental decisions.

The corporatist trends within British government are reinforced by the logic and style of decision-making found in the EEC. For instance, within the treaties that establish the EEC farming and agricultural policy, there are specific requirements for the relevant economic interest groups to be formally incorporated. The NFU is thus very well represented in Brussels.

Environmental groups are in general more likely to be incorporated into the politically marginal and less powerful government agencies. This is not true of the National Farmers' Union. There was no dissent in the interviews carried out for the *Politics of Pressure* from the view that the NFU and the Ministry of Agriculture, Fisheries and Food (MAFF) work very closely together. Des Wilson notes:

> 'Very often there is no difference whatsoever in the

noises that come from the spokesman of the NFU and from the Ministry of Agriculture.'

In a comparative analysis of British and American farmers' lobby styles, Graham Wilson makes the following point in his book *Special Interests and Policymaking* (1977):

'The British NFU's leaders have used their autonomy to maintain close and friendly relations with government in general and MAFF in particular. They have behaved less politically, more moderately, and more like an extension of the Civil Service than many of their members would have wished ...'

The NFU, through its close relations with government, is able to acquire advance intelligence about new developments and so has the time to respond. To its advantage and the consequent disadvantage of its opponents, the NFU is brought in at an early and formative stage in the discussion of new proposals. Conservation and environmental groups complain that the Wildlife and Countryside Bill of 1981 illustrates the advantages gained by a lobby group with incorporated status in that the main outlines of the Bill were decided amongst ministers, senior civil servants, the leaders of the National Farmers' Union and the Country Landowners' Association before the Bill was finally drafted.

There is little doubt that this close relationship gives the NFU influence which is the envy of other groups and a source of frustration to those who see farming interests dominating countryside issues. Ian Brotherton of Sheffield University argues that representatives of agricultural interests have increased on the boards of committees of the National Parks. Since the Conservative Government of 1979 agricultural representation on such boards has increased by 50 per cent. Brotherton also points out that since 1980 56 per cent of ministerial appointments have been from among those in 'farming and related activities' with a corresponding decline in representation from groups concerned with conservation and recreation in our National Parks.

Apart from its lobbying skill as an organisation, what is the source of the NFU's political influence? Unlike many industrial organisations it is not large, nor is it economically concentrated as are the manufacturing, commercial and financial institutions in Britain. Its influence can be explained by a number of factors. One factor is its incorporation into any decision-making which has resulted directly from EEC policy-making processes. Another is its contacts within the Conservative Party. Des Wilson explains:

'The source of their power is first of all in the nature of the Conservative Party. Don't forget until recently there were nine members of the Cabinet who owned farms. I mean, imagine that – a Cabinet room full of men and women who own farms. What chance have you got of challenging a power-base like that? Secondly, you've got a Ministry that has been working with the NFU for so long that they talk the same language; they go to the same clubs and eat in the same restaurants. They know each other on first-name terms. At this moment, although Friends of the Earth has done all the research on pesticides ... the Government is talking to farmers and the chemical industry in formulating legislative plans. They're not talking to us, we are not on the inside there, we are not part of the club.'

In addition, and crucially, according to Philip Lowe, the source of the NFU's power does not come simply from its access to the Conservative Party; after all, farmers have also been incorporated into the policy-formulating process under Labour Governments. He believes that the NFU's influential status as an insider group in the Department of Agriculture derives from the agricultural policies pursued by all governments since the Second World War. Since the war British Governments have been committed to intervention in farming, but in a form which did not require the nationalisation of land. Farming was left in the hands of a set of small private operators. Philip Lowe:

'Now if one was going to have a system in which one is going to have the most regulated sector of the British economy, which is what agriculture is, with the State most involved but still with elements of private enterprise and private property, then arguably the only way one could do that is by an intimate relationship between the economic interest group which represents the farmers, i.e. the National Farmers' Union, and the government set up to manage agriculture, i.e. the Ministry of Agriculture.'

He argues that the power of the National Farmers' Union emanates from this style of public intervention. In other words:

> 'It isn't that the National Farmers' Union has a lot of economic power which determines a strong relationship with Government, but that the strong relationship with Government gives the National Farmers' Union its power.'

The major advantage for those groups brought into the corporatist style of decision-making is that they gain access to decision-makers and can influence their decisions. However, there are disadvantages. By staying outside the system groups may acquire more flexibility and freedom of action. Their teeth are not drawn by their proximity to those who pull the strings.

Pluralism
Pluralists believe that the lobbying activity of pressure groups, interest organisations and voluntary associations is one of the crucial factors in defining and maintaining an effective democracy. At the end of Chapter 1 I listed six reasons for arguing that lobbying is beneficial for a democracy. Briefly summarised here again, the reasons are: monitoring government; providing information; representing minorities; giving an alternative mode of political participation; offering counter-pressures to other powerful groups; and providing stimuli to political debate.

Dr Geoffrey Alderman of the University of London is convinced that pressure groups are an asset to the democratic process in that they accommodate more people with divergent views and allow them to play a part in the political system. He says:

> 'Far more people in this country are involved in the re-ordering of society through their involvement in pressure groups than through their involvement in political parties or putting a cross on a ballot-paper once every five years. Pressure groups are a way of involving more people in the running of the country, and that is very important as an ingredient in the social cement of this country. People will not accept laws

simply because Parliament passed them. They will accept laws because they believe they have had some input into the framing of them.'

Lobby groups can help to overcome three weaknesses in our parliamentary form of government: rule by the majority to the detriment of the minority; short-term thinking in government; and ineffective opposition in Parliament. Those factors are crucial, according to Des Wilson, if we are to appreciate the true worth of lobby groups in our system of government. He says:

'In my view you have to acknowledge that there are weaknesses in democracy. The first is, by definition, a rule by the majority and that means there are minorities whom the system does not serve. Secondly, our form of democracy means our leaders must, at fairly short intervals, return to be re-elected and re-appointed. In order to get our applause and to be re-elected they have to come up with results in a short period of time. Now this means that thinking and actions tend to be short-term, whereas many of our problems require a long-term approach.'

It is Des Wilson's lack of faith in a third aspect of British parliamentary democracy – the failure of the political parties – which is the basis of what he sees as another advantage of pluralist politics:

'I don't regard pressure groups as one factor in the democratic process. I regard us as a vital, central and necessary factor who are actually making a democratic process democratic, because I believe we are the official opposition. To me, all of the major political parties are part of the same governmental system. If you take some of the causes I've been fighting: no party acted on lead in petrol until our campaign made it happen; no party introduced freedom of information, although they have all had the same opportunity.'

A further benefit of the pluralist form of politics is that lobby groups can provide alternative sources of information to the official statements on public policy. By concentrating its efforts, a lobby group can effectively scan public statements and so monitor what is being universally said; become recognised as the relevant agency to contact with new or leaked information; promote its own research and so generate new data; and become established as a source of reliable information and specialist intelligence for both public and politicians. Lobby groups are, as Des Wilson states:

> 'Far more knowledgeable than any one MP can be who has a dozen and one things to do every day. Pressure groups, by concentrating on specific subjects, become knowledgeable and provide a form of expert surveillance over what the authorities are doing.'

Pressure groups can also help to keep issues alive and part of the political agenda. They can given an issue stamina according to Wilson:

> 'Newspapers and TV pick up issues, ride them for a few days, then drop them again. The pressure group hangs on in there day after day, week after week, month after month, year after year, perpetuating that issue and developing that issue and giving it a stamina which means there is some chance of it not getting lost.'

Finally, pressure groups provide a counter-balance to powerful groups in society. This is called counter-vailing power. Lobby groups can combat the activities of other pressure groups. As Des Wilson points out:

> '. . . not all pressure groups are good, some of them are extremely evil, and some of them are very, very powerful . . . a lot of them are interested in their own personal gain and profit, and pressure groups exist to combat them, like the National Farmers' Union, which has succeeded in perpetuating in this country the most outrageously generous deal towards farmers and the most appalling economic and agricultural policies with virtually no opposition. So pressure groups like Friends of the Earth emerge and one of their key roles is to oppose those very powerful pressure groups.'

There are some supporters of a more pluralistic form of government, such as Michael Young, who see within it potential dangers. As interest-articulation expands on a broadening number of particular issues, how is the system to accommodate all its differing demands? Such accommodation is especially difficult if this expansion coincides with the decline of a more general mobilisation based on political parties which previously have, through a series of compromises, reached some level of accommodation between competing claims made on governmental time and resources. Michael Young:

'... the danger, as I see it, is that emotional energy will be abstracted from the political parties. The loyalties and enthusiasm that they could command in the past will no longer be there for them, but they will be swept up in a series of large and small pluralistic crusades. If that happens and continues to happen, as it appears to be, then people could stop being interested in ordinary politics.'

A second criticism of the pluralistic view of power is that it overlooks the imbalance which exists between the competing lobby groups. Counter-vailing power is not a reality in a society where some sections of the community have disproportionate control over economic resources, social status and political power.

Dr Geoffrey Alderman has noted this problem:

'Certainly there is an imbalance, there is a question of differential access. Some pressure groups are extraordinarily privileged, they are bedded down snugly with government departments in a way which could not be undone without destroying parts of the government machinery.'

Counter-mobilisation and campaigning require money, an effective organisation and access to the influential decision-makers and opinion-leaders. The political underdogs – pensioners, immigrants, non-unionised labour – are bound to be less influential than those sectors with wealth and political clout.

A third criticism of pluralism is whether those who speak on behalf of organisations truly represent the members of those organisations. As Robert Michels noted in his analysis of German democratic political parties, the leadership may not accurately represent the views of the membership. His book *Political Parties*, first published in 1908, showed how bureaucratic and democratic requirements within a party organisation helped to distort the original organisational goals and led to a distancing between leaders and the membership. His analysis applies as aptly to lobby groups as it does to political parties.

The relevance for a pluralist theory of government is obvious. If pressure groups and interest groups mobilise people, kccp issues alive, provide an alternative and radical version of events and form the real opposition to the Government, then democracy can only be served so long as the policies put forward by organisations reflect the views of their members.

Some parliamentarians complain that lobby groups distort the public interest by not attempting to identify the general interest of the community. Instead they pursue, single-mindedly, sectional interests. Those who see Parliament as the cornerstone of our democracy are less ready to admit that lobby groups, as Des Wilson suggests, provide the 'vital, central and necessary factor' for democracy.

In Samuel Brittan's book *The Role and Limits of Government*, published in 1983, he argues that interest groups are tyrannical and insensitive to the needs of the wider public; they are, he claims, far from indispensable. In December 1983 Lord Hailsham, during the debate on the Matrimonial and Family Proceedings Bill, described the pressure groups involved in lobbying against the Bill as 'deliberately cruel' because of their attempt to mobilise support by unsettling and upsetting people who could not be adversely affected by the Bill. In the 1983 BBC TV series *Honourable Members*, Jo Grimmond MP bemoaned the vast increase in bureaucracy not only in Whitehall but also amongst pressure groups. 'Today's back-bench MP', he declared, 'is swamped by circulars from every conceivable sort of pressure group, including The One-Fingered Irish Association of West Houghton.'

Larry Gostin, an American, worked as a civil rights lawyer in Washington before becoming the director of MIND from 1974 to 1983, and then director of the NCCL in 1983. He distinguishes the contrasting roles played by lobby groups in the USA and Britain as the difference between distortion by influence, and policy change through persuasion.

'In America it really is pressure group politics in the very worst sense of the word where you have to be somebody who can wield influence, ... you have to win by power, rather than by persuasion and winning the argument. Whereas in this country I think there is a great deal to be proud of because winning the argument is much more important. If you are able to put forward cogent arguments [and] good briefing material, it will be picked up and appreciated by MPs and the public and will be well reported and that is the characteristic I think of pressure group and voluntary organisations in this country.'

Burkean democracy

In contrast to those who consider that democracy is either served by the incorporation of differing interests into government, or by allowing competition between a plurality of lobby groups to generate public policy, there are those who adopt the view that democracy only operates through a system of parliamentary representation in which the representatives consider not sectional but national interests. This view of British democracy was first proposed by the eighteenth-century MP for Bristol and political philosopher, Edmund Burke.

In his address to the electors of Bristol at the time of his election to Parliament in 1774, Burke said:

'Parliament is not a congress of ambassadors from different and hostile interests; which interests each must maintain, as agent and advocate, against other agents and advocates; but Parliament is a deliberative assembly of one nation, with one interest, that of the whole; where, not local prejudices ought to guide, but the general good, resulting from the general reason of the whole. You choose a Member indeed; but when you have chosen him, he is not a Member of Bristol, but he is a Member of Parliament.'

Patrick Cormack MP quotes Burke to explain what he considers to be the role of a Member of Parliament:

'Manifestos are general expressions of general intent and no Member of Parliament is bound to every last dot in a manifesto. MPs are not puppets on strings which are pulled by outside organisations.'

The Burkean view of politics identifies Parliament as the arbiter of the national interest – overcoming and reconciling short-term and sectional interests which might be encouraged by lobby groups. Furthermore, MPs are in a better position than ministers to judge 'the best interests of the nation'. Ministers are too far removed from the realities of life. Patrick Cormack again:

> 'I think Secretaries of State ... are often remote creatures wrapped in cotton wool and surrounded by civil servants, whisked from meeting to meeting in limousines, who don't always fully comprehend what life is all about.'

Critics of the Burkean view of politics disagree primarily with the elitist assumption about the paramount role attributed to the representative and the meagre part attributed to the citizen who appears on stage only at election times. Secondly, they claim that the present parliamentary system does not allow MPs any degree of autonomy, nor encourage any independence of mind *vis-à-vis* long-term national interests that Burke asserted they should have. This occurs for three reasons: firstly, the parties' stranglehold over MPs, represented by the power of the whips; secondly, the uneven balance between Parliament and the executive – the Prime Minister has become a much more powerful figure; and thirdly, the scope and complexity of modern government which makes it difficult for MPs to comprehend the details of government, other than at the most superficial level. Des Wilson comments:

> 'I lost my faith in Members of Parliament as free crusaders a long time ago ... I would say that ... in 1985 the role of most Conservative MPs will be to vote for what Mrs Thatcher wants them to vote for. To call them the conscience of a democracy would be absurd.'

Hilary Jackson also thinks that democracy requires the wider involvement of the community and asserts that MPs and Parliament do not have a monopoly on good ideas:

> 'We operate in a parliamentary democracy that is not about, hopefully, a vote once every four or five years. It is about being constantly active, persuasive and persistent in persuading people of your views, and that

action takes place outside Parliament. We certainly don't think Parliament has some infinite wisdom and knowledge about how our society should be organised.'

2.4 *'Hands Off Hook!'*

In the first part of this chapter I looked at the activities and organisations of some national lobby groups concerned with the use of the countryside, and then discussed three theories which attempt to explain the relevance of lobby groups in British politics. In the last section of this chapter I shall focus on a recent controversy about the green belt and planning laws. The conflict involved established interest groups, emphasis groups and principle pressure groups, and a spontaneous protest group which was formed to prevent a massive building development in the village of Hook in Hampshire. In considering this issue I shall refer to the three theories of power already described – corporatist, pluralist and Burkean – and assess how they impinged on the controversy.

In 1983 the House Builders' Federation (HBF), which represents most of the country's major commercial housebuilding firms, claimed that, as the result of a survey it had conducted, almost a third of the sites in the metropolitan green belt were serving no 'useful' green belt purpose. The clear message to the Government was that these sites, several of them clearly under-used, should be released for housing development. The HBF then demanded in the summer of 1983 an urgent review of green belt policy, alleging that it was pushing up house prices excessively and keeping first-time buyers out of the housing market.

Then came the announcement that a consortium of 10 of the country's largest housebuilding companies intended to construct a ring of 15 new 'villages' around London. The first announcement of this dramatic new development came at a conference organised by Berkshire CPRE in July, 1983. Tom Baron, Chairman of the Volume Housebuilders, told the conference that several of these proposed 'villages' would require green field locations to provide 7000–8000 houses. Later it became clear that up to a third of the villages would be located in the metropolitan green belt.

In July and August of 1983 the Department of the Environment published two draft circulars: *Land for Housing* and *Memorandum on Structure and Local Plans and Green Belt*. These indicated the Government's position on this issue and proved to be the first major departure from countryside planning policy as laid down by the Town and Country Planning Act since its enactment in 1947. It allowed greater freedom to develop green field sites away from the cities. The *Land for Housing* circular stated that even where local authorities could show they held a supply of housing land sufficient for seven years' construction, this was no longer a sufficient reason for refusing permission for other sites considered to be more 'readily available' for development.

The second draft circular about green belt policy was also a shock to local conservation groups. The circular envisaged a more relaxed attitude towards building development within the green belt zone. This they regarded as a concession to the demands of the commercial housebuilders.

The environmental lobby proclaimed its opposition to the draft circulars. First of all, informal links were established, and taking the lead was the CPRE. Des Wilson explains why the FOE took a backseat role on this issue:

> 'It is a very interesting example of horses for courses where the right pressure group was the Council for the Protection of Rural England, a conservative organisation who are more comfortable talking to Conservatives.'

Robin Grove-White, the Director of CPRE, explains the spearhead role played by his organisation:

> 'We have been concerned for three or four years about the drift of government policy towards control over development in rural areas and local authority control over patterns of development because that has a lot of implications for the countryside. When these two draft circulars were published, it was quite clear to us that these were something of a watershed, because they would have signalled to the building lobby that they were going to get their own way from the Government very much more strongly than in the past. That was

why we put a lot of effort into campaigning against
them, and we worked in harmony with the local
authority associations, the NFU, the Civic Trust and
other organisations. We were the public face of the
campaign, if you like, but we were dovetailing what we
were doing very much with what they were doing.'

As a result of the lobbying, Patrick Jenkin, the Secretary of
State for the Environment, withdrew his proposals. CPRE
organised a major conference in London, the audience of
which comprised 400 people from green belt local
authorities. They were given assurances by the Secretary of
State himself that the green belt policy was safe with him.

The interests at stake were not just those affecting the
environmental lobby. There was another division of interest
between the small and the volume housebuilders, both of
whom have influence within the Conservative Party. This
was because the new departures heralded by the draft
circulars were likely to be of more benefit to the volume
housebuilders, particularly the new conglomerate of Consortium Developments, than to the small housebuilders
since it was proposed that the land would be released in very
large chunks. The existing system of planning laws, under
which small amounts of land for the purpose of new buildings are released gradually, usually worked more to the
advantage of the smaller building company.

The directors of smaller companies are well entrenched in
local rural politics, particularly within the Conservative
Party, and are well represented at both county and district
level. But the influence of the HBF was exercised through its
contacts with central government and in particular the
Department of the Environment. Tom Baron, spokesman
for Consortium Developments, had worked as a political
adviser at the Department of the Environment under a previous Conservative minister. He is now a Director of
Christian Salveson, which, along with the following nine
volume housebuilding companies, makes up Consortium
Developments: Barratt, Bovis, Brosaley, Comber, John
MacLaine, New Ideal Holdings, Wilcon, Wimpey and
William Leach.

The division of interest between large and small builder
was overlaid by two ideological stands – monetarism and

paternalism – both of which flourish in the Conservative Government and Party. Doctrinal points were brought into play: on the one hand to justify a reduction in the use of planning laws, and less government intervention and greater freedom for market forces; and on the other to demand a greater voice for local interests, conservation of the countryside and the pursuit of public interest before profit-making.

The lobby groups decided that a key tactic was to mobilise backbench Conservative MPs. Robin Grove-White:

> 'It was quite obvious to us that the key to the whole thing lay in the Conservative backbenches and many of the constituencies that would be affected most directly by these circulars would be ones which had Conservative Members of Parliament. We were absolutely specific about who we encouraged to sign an Early Day Motion in the House of Commons and they were backbench Tories. To be absolutely candid about it, we didn't bother with the Labour Party. They would like to see houses built on green belt land, and that is why we let the Council for the Protection of Rural England give the lead on that, because it's a more conservative campaign group than Friends of the Earth.'

Julian Critchley, MP for Aldershot, was one of the local Conservative MPs affected by the proposed development in Hook by Consortium Developments. In the House of Commons he put down an Early Day Motion and a hundred Conservative Members of Parliament signed it. He explains what happened next:

> 'Now, when a backbencher has a piece of paper with the signatures of 99 of his fellow Members of Parliament on it he can march into the Whips' Office and put the fear of God up the Government, and it means that you are wafted straightaway in a black ministerial motor car to see Patrick Jenkin, the "great man".'

The result was that both the 1983 draft circulars were withdrawn and a victory on the green belt seemed secure. The Minister, Patrick Jenkin, expressed himself thus in the pages of the *Sunday Times*:

> 'I have stated many times that I remain fully committed to a strong, permanent green belt policy.'

Yet a year later the re-issue of the *Land for Housing* circular has aroused concern again. This document still hints at greater central Government intervention to over-rule local councils' 'Land Structure' plans. The feeling in the village of Hook is that Consortium Developments could still get the Department of the Environment's approval to build a mini-village there and over-rule local opinion and the Hampshire County Council's 'Structure Plan'.

So more action is being taken. Hook village have organised a 'Hands Off Hook Action Group'. Local council-lors from Hart District Council, which also opposes the new circulars, are joining the fight. Peter Duckworth and Bill Baggs have given the lead and the three local Conservative MPs – Julian Critchley, Andrew Hunter and Michael Mates – turned up to speak to a meeting of worried villagers in July 1984.

Despite the support of a long list of official public organis-ations like the County Councils Association, and promo-tional and emphasis lobby groups like FOE and CPRE, there is still obvious anxiety in Hook that Consortium Develop-ments will get its way because of its huge resources and its influence in the Department of the Environment. Bill Baggs, organiser of the 'Hands Off Hook Campaign' expresses his pessimism:

> 'Initially, I was delighted when draft Circular X/83 was withdrawn. In fact, I was quoted in the local press as saying it was the happiest day since England won the World Cup. But I am afraid that delight was short-lived because Circular X/84 came along in draft form and we believe it was only a revamping of Circular X/83. It spelt out the same things that X/83 did in as much that the Secretary of State would allow new settlements in certain situations.
>
> Consortium Developments have been placed on record as saying they are prepared to spend half a mil-lion pounds on each planning appeal to ensure that they win it. We at Hook can come nowhere near that figure.'

In terms of the three views of democracy discussed earlier, it is clear that on this issue corporatist, pluralist and Burkean tendencies were in evidence. The corporatists can claim that the initial circulars were very much shaped by the House-builders' Federation through their access to, and incorporation into, key decision-making bodies within the Department of the Environment. The conflict over the two circulars demonstrates the role that lobby organisations can play and illustrates the pluralist claim that pressure-group activity can achieve results. Government policy remains in a state of flux while mobilisation and counter-mobilisation takes place, thus illustrating the nature of counter-vailing power. The Burkeans can find some satisfaction from the fact that it was pressure from the Early Day Motion in Parliament which influenced the Secretary of State's decision to withdraw the two draft circulars.

But the battle is not yet over, as Julian Critchley explains:

'The housebuilders have lots of money and they are prepared to spend it. They also have the added advantage that many people who live in our cities wish to come and live in suburban and rural areas such as parts of Aldershot, Hampshire and Surrey. So they have the demand, and they have the money. What stops them building houses wherever they would like to build houses and sell them is, of course, the whole of the planning laws. The planning laws are administered by local government in conjunction with the Department of the Environment, but they have to work to rules laid down by the Department of the Environment. If the Department of the Environment is prepared to change the rules in favour of the housebuilders, then of course they win the battle. What we have managed to do so far is to keep the rules as they were before.'

In addition, the emergence of a village pressure group in Hook shows that more people can be encouraged to participate in political issues through lobbying on behalf of a single issue than are likely to join or participate in a political party.

[In November 1984 I heard from a jubilant Julian Critchley that Consortium Developments had withdrawn its plan to build a mini-village in Hook.]

3 *Lobbying Westminster*

In this chapter I shall be looking at the part Parliament and parliamentarians – both in the House of Commons and the House of Lords – play in the process of lobbying. How useful are MPs? Is it worth hiring a professional public relations firm to promote your cause in Parliament? How have some lobby groups managed to sponsor successful private Members' bills? I shall look at one such bill affecting the solicitors' conveyancing monopoly and examine the lobbying strategies used by the Consumers' Association who sponsored the bill and the Law Society who opposed it. How party ideology influences lobbying will also be discussed, as will the efforts by lobby groups to influence elections to Parliament. Finally I shall look at the occasions when MPs find themselves more influential than usual as, for instance, when they have a free vote on some matter.

Every lobby organisation, before it deals with Parliament, needs to know to what extent, on what occasions, and in what circumstances Parliament is powerful. One view about the relative importance of Parliament is given by Andrew Roth, an American who set up his company, Parliamentary Profiles, to provide biographical details of British politicians. His office is in Palace Chambers, a block shared with the Foreign Office, and is located across the street from Parliament in Bridge Street.

> 'Across the street in Parliament they decide all sorts of things. Whether it's teachers' pay or nurses' pay or what's happening to opticians or what's happening to solicitors. Unless people take an intelligent close view of what's happening over there they can be caught by surprise – sometimes to their disadvantage.'

The Labour MP Geoffrey Robinson, who has been in the House of Commons since 1976, adds a cautionary comment about the scope and nature of Parliament's influence.

Speaking from the viewpoint of an opposition backbencher he says:

> 'Our powers are very limited; we can only win the argument. But it's the process of debate and the cut and thrust of politics that is important over a period of a Parliament. If you continue to win the argument it can demoralise the Government quite considerably and change the general trends of its policies. Not in the early stages, but over a Parliament of three or four years, ministers are ground down by having to present policies and defend policies in which many of them just don't believe.'

3.1 *Working with MPs*

How can MPs help a lobby organisation? Essentially they provide a channel to those in power and help to get a topic raised publicly; they provide access to those with influence in government and help set the agenda of public debate. More rarely, they can achieve legislative success via private Members' legislation.

This is theoretically possible through the Friday afternoon sessions kept available for bills from backbench MPs and also through the 'ten minute rule' procedure. But more routinely they can ask questions in the House of Commons and provide information.

Des Wilson sees the function of MPs as being able 'to pull some strings'. Ministers are much more likely to reply quickly and carefully if an enquiry comes from an MP.

> 'Sometimes a Member of Parliament will come to a pressure group like the Freedom of Information campaign and say: "I wish to get the water authorities re-opened because now they're all operating in secret. Is your campaign interested? Could you present me with a draft bill? What do you suggest are the kind of questions I should be tabling? Is there anything I can do in the House?". That would help and that's marvellous; we sit down and work it out together. We provide,

if you like, a service to that MP. Sometimes we will go
to an MP and say: "Look, we want to introduce a piece
of legislation under the 'ten minute rule' procedure,
we know you have a record on this from what you said
in debates or from what you said in a newspaper
article." It's arranged that way.'

Although chances of success are very low, private
Members' bills do sometimes become enacted, as with
David Steel's Abortion Bill in 1967. They can also provide
a fillip to government action as with Austin Mitchell's
House Buyers Bill. These two examples illustrate an MP
working in co-operation with a lobby organisation, which
will provide the background research and information
necessary for the bill. The lobby group can also help on a
private Member's bill by rallying the support of other sympathetic MPs at division times in Parliament and acting as
a sort of unofficial whip.

Another ploy used by lobby groups is to get as many MPs
as possible to give support to a campaign. Des Wilson:

'With my campaigns I like to submit to every backbench MP our objectives and explain what they're
about. We invite them to put their name to the campaign and this gives the media, the Government and
others, some indication of the kind of political support
the issue's got. If you take the case of lead in petrol,
we ended up with over 200 Members of Parliament
listed in our material as supporters. The Campaign
for Freedom of Information has got about 175 MPs and
about 50 members of the House of Lords. Now that's
very helpful in indicating political support.'

But the first step in the 'partnership' (Des Wilson's word)
between MP and lobby group, is to identify those MPs who
are sympathetic. Andrew Bennett MP puts the views of the
Ramblers' Association. Julian Critchley MP is pleased to
speak in defence of NATO's interests without payment,
because he believes in them. Lobby groups might be disappointed at times when MPs express their private support but
refuse to act publicly on behalf of a campaign. Michael
Schofield found this out at the time of the lobbying for
homosexual reforms and the campaign to legalise
cannabis:

'MPs are important [but] they're not as important as they think they are. There are two levels of morality with MPs. I wouldn't say they're all hypocritical. I suppose all of us have a private face and public activities. But the homosexual lobby will always tell you that the gay MPs would never initiate any homosexual law reform. With cannabis, we knew of a few MPs who had the occasional joint but we could never get them to make the first move.'

Julian Critchley warns against one basic mistake made by lobby groups when approaching parliamentarians: avoid depersonalised mass mailing of circular letters in brown envelopes with a second class stamp and the company's or campaign's name on the front. These tend to be despatched to the waste-paper bin unopened. Mary Whitehouse organises her write-in campaigns carefully to avoid this:

'I know that some pressure groups for instance have a circular-style letter. We never do that. When we write letters to the papers we suggest people write in their own terms, in their own way, as they see fit personally to their MP. Now no MP worth his salt or who cares about his seat is going to ignore personal letters written like that.'

As for selecting a sympathetic MP, some carry more weight than others. A general rule is that government backbenchers are better than opposition ones, and the more senior the better. Some MPs should be actively avoided according to Julian Critchley:

'For God's sake don't approach y and z because the rest of us think that they are mad and you would be wasting your time if you got them to speak out for you. I mean there are well known Members of Parliament who are at the end of everyone's telephone. Every sub-editor who wants to cry "Disgusted, Says Mr X" knows you can ring up Mr X. Well, there is many a cause that is never finally lost until Mr X has made it his own, and you have to identify who they are.'

That government rather than opposition MPs have more influence simply reflects the shifting balance of power away from Westminster to Whitehall, so that MPs with access to,

and contacts in, government departments and the Prime
Minister's Office are what a lobby group would most prize.
Julian Critchley explains:

> 'Most Members of Parliament do not have power. In
> combination they may have a good deal of influence
> but very few of us have power. I mean the whole pur-
> pose of being a backbench Member of Parliament on
> the government side is to sustain the Government in
> office.'

Julian Critchley's advice to lobby groups is to find a sympathetic, influential, senior, government backbencher, like
Edward du Cann. He is not so certain of the benefits of *paying*
for an MP to act as a lobby group spokesman in the way that
Eldon Griffiths is paid to represent the Police Federation.

> 'The Police Federation employs Mr Eldon Griffiths.
> He is known in the House as "Constable Griffiths" who
> rises to his feet with great regularity whenever any
> matter appertaining to law and order is being debated.
> When Mr Griffiths gets up yet again the rest of us MPs
> are inclined to groan slightly because we know he is
> doing something for which he is being paid, but having
> said that, he does, I think, a good job for the police.'

Although 'Constable Griffiths' might make MPs moan, the
Police Federation know that the journalists in the press gallery, particularly those from the *Daily Mail*, the *Sun* and the
Daily Express, are only too pleased to report on police issues,
especially if it is one serious enough to have been raised
publicly in the House of Commons. 'Constable Griffiths' can
help via the press gallery to get police issues and the Police
Federation's views across to a wider audience than the
House of Commons.

The Police Federation are not the only interest group to
have MPs working to secure them a voice on public issues.
The tobacco lobby is another powerful group that operates
successfully with the help of MPs. Mike Daube estimates that
there are three or four directly on the pay-roll of tobacco
companies, such as Sir Anthony Kershaw who is paid by
British American Tobacco. Other MPs are less obviously
linked to the industry through public relations and consultancy firms hired by tobacco companies, so their involvement goes unrecorded in the Register of Members' Interests.

How do such MPs help to promote or protect the interests of the tobacco industry? Firstly they have the general advantage of being able to obtain information on relevant issues from government departments (in this case the Department of Trade and the Department of Health and Social Security), and in addition they can speak up for the industry in debates in the House.

A third advantage is explained by Mike Daube. It involves their skill in exploiting parliamentary procedures to stop unfavourable legislation from going through.

'There is the procedural work they do, and that can be everything from messing about with early day motions to actually talking out bills. ... They put down so many amendments that the bill you want doesn't get parliamentary time. Sir John Langford-Holt, who was a Tory MP and a consultant to Imperial Tobacco, spoke 10 times before a debate on tobacco was due to be reached and managed to prevent the debate from being reached but he didn't have to declare an interest while he was speaking on the other subject.'

On 12 June 1981, a day set aside for private Members' bills, Sir Anthony Kershaw tabled 27 out of 164 trivial amendments to the Zoo Licensing Bill. The sudden interest in zoos had to do with the subsequent item that day, which was a bill proposed by Laurie Pavitt to eliminate tobacco sponsorship for sport and the arts. Pavitt's bill was not debated owing to lack of time.

Effective lobbying will also require MPs to engage in horse-trading behind the scenes so that a promise to support another lobby group's interest will ensure their support for yours. The network of lobbying between MPs will, if successful, involve the Whips' Office so that the Government will know of the degrees of support for its proposals in the House of Commons. Sir George Young, a Minister in the Department of Health and Social Security from 1979 to 1981, tried to promote measures that would reduce cigarette smoking and became the target of behind the scenes efforts by MPs sympathetic to the tobacco lobby to get him moved. This came to the attention of the whips who informed the Prime Minister. Young was subsequently moved.

Another example of an MP who has worked closely with a lobby group is David Myles, a former NFU official in Scotland. He became an MP and represented Banff between 1979–83, and co-operated closely with the NFU officials at Agriculture House – the premises of the NFU. In particular he kept in contact with one full-time official, Barney Holbeche, who co-ordinates the efforts of the NFU lobby at Westminster. One strategy he favoured was making use of Parliamentary Question Time. Supposedly an opportunity to expose the Government to ruthless cross-examination, it is more often used by MPs to remind a minister that a lobby organisation has an interest on a topic. In addition, by asking questions MPs can help to mobilise support both in and out of Parliament. This might be in collusion with a minister who prefers there to be a groundswell of parliamentary support before taking action. As David Myles explains:

'The minister cannot really do anything by himself in Parliament, he needs a swell of parliamentary opinion behind him and therefore it's very important to get an adequate number of MPs who will actually promote and push this kind of support. . . . A lot of the time, you see, Members of Parliament are so busy they really don't have time to think of the question that would be relevant . . . I would say to MPs: "Do you want to ask a question of the Minister of Agriculture?" If they said "yes", I'd say, "Which one do you want?" and give them a choice and, of course, each Member only had one question. And Barney Holbeche helped me a bit. I used to tell him, "Look, send me all the questions you want asked, and I will ensure that some of them will be asked". I can remember one MP being greatly pleased because once . . . I got him to ask a question on Aujesky's disease [a disease of pigs]. When he came up on the ballot, he came up to me and said: "For God's sake tell me what the hell I am going to ask as a supplementary question. I dunno what Aujesky's disease is." So I had to learn too, to find out what exactly it was and what would be the line. So I had to phone up Barney Holbeche to ask what line he would like taken on Aujesky's disease. This fellow then asked a supplementary question and got quite an illuminating answer. Then all the farming press were phoning him up. He suddenly became an expert on Aujesky's disease. This is the way it works.'

Apart from farming interests, David Myles was expected to speak on matters effecting the 35 whisky distilleries in his constituency of Banff:

'With 35 distilleries they were one of my big constituency interests. During Geoffrey Howe's last budget day I was sitting in the Chamber listening to the budget debate when I got a note handed in from the Scottish Whisky Association . . . I went out to see them, and they said: "We've got a brief here we would desperately like to be put across in the budget debate". I went away and queued at the Speaker's chair to ask if I could get a spot in the budget debate, and just by chance Maurice Macmillan was standing in front of me. Through our involvement in Europe we were quite friendly. He turned to me and said: "You go in front of me because I only want to withdraw". I said: "No, if you're going to withdraw you go in front of me", and he, of course, was a senior Member who had a spot in the debate. He asked if he could withdraw and immediately I went in and the Speaker said: "I just happen to have a spot, Maurice Macmillan's spot", and he put me in and I was able to talk more or less on the brief that I'd got from the Scottish Whisky Association.'

3.2 Private Members' legislation

A lobby group's dream is to be given the chance of putting forward a proposal to Parliament to be considered for legislation. The only real opportunity for this, unless the Government can be persuaded to adopt it, is through the procedure known as the private Member's bill. This allows backbenchers to introduce legislation into the House of Commons. The chances of its being enacted are small, unless the Government is prepared to give it time and tacit approval, as happened with David Steel's Abortion Bill in 1967 and the Murder (Abolition of the Death Penalty) Bill of 1965. The chance to introduce a bill by this means is decided by a ballot between backbench MPs, that is the 400 out of 650 MPs who are not also part of the Government or the official Opposition. Only the top 10 in any one year have much chance of getting a bill introduced as only up to 10 Fridays in each annual session are set aside for private Members' bills.

John Corrie, MP for Cunningham North in Scotland, has been successful twice in the last few years in the ballots in 1979/80 and 1982/3. In 1979 he introduced the Abortion (Amendment) Bill which was sponsored by a number of lobby groups such as the Society for the Protection of the Unborn Child who thought the existing legislation encouraged too many abortions. John Corrie did not have a peaceful year in that parliamentary session as he was badgered continually by both opponents and supporters of the bill. His bill was defeated despite widespread public support from well organised lobby groups, mainly because the proposers were unwilling to compromise over the detail of the bill, and there was strong opposition both in Parliament and the country. It was noticeable that when Corrie had the extremely rare good fortune to be high in the ballot in the 1982/3 session of Parliament, he did not choose to introduce another bill on abortion.

Mary Whitehouse (NVALA) and David Tench (Consumers' Association) have both had successes with private Members' bills concerning video censorship and the solicitors' conveyancing monopoly on house purchases respectively. These experienced campaigners know the importance of being around when the private Members' ballot is announced. David Tench explains the origins of the House Buyers Bill proposed by Austin Mitchell, MP for Grimsby:

'We have found over the years that the private Members' ballot, which happens in every parliamentary year, is a very good way of getting issues into Parliament and, indeed, of changing the law from time to time. So every year when the ballot is drawn, almost as soon as the Queen has opened Parliament, we reckon to have an issue that we can put before the MPs who have drawn a place in the ballot and we say, "What about this one? How about taking up this issue? If you take it up we'll help you." So in June of 1983, just after the General Election when the new session had started we thought, "What shall we do this time?" And since we had over the years expressed a lot of dissatisfaction in *Which?* and elsewhere about the house transfer system as we call it, we thought, "Let's have a go at that again". So we devised a proposal to remove the monopoly that solicitors have on conveyancing ... and sent it to each of the MPs who drew a place in the ballot. Now, one of the techniques we've found is that it pays to be quick off the mark so that I, for example, actually go to the ballot when it's drawn at 12.00 on the day in question and rush back the half a mile from Parliament to my office immediately after the ballot and get the word processor moving. By an hour and a half after the ballot is drawn, letters are actually going into the House of Commons post office and into the pigeon holes of the 20 MPs who have drawn a place in the ballot. That is intended to impress them that we know what we're doing and are quick off the mark. Mrs Whitehouse of course also knows this technique. She is inclined to grab people by the hand as soon as she can find them and say, "What about my issue?" That's one of the techniques of lobbying – to be quick off the mark. Then you just sit back and wait for any one of the 20 to get in touch with you and say, "I'm mildly interested." In June of 1983 nothing much happened and the last day for putting in the proposals came and I concluded that this was going to be one of our fallow years and nothing would happen. About 2.00 in the afternoon the telephone goes and it's Mr Austin Mitchell who says, "They tell me I've got to get my proposal in by 5.00, I haven't really decided yet. Didn't you send me something? What do you think I should do?" So I said, "I'll be with you in 5 minutes."'

During the 1983 General Election campaign Mary Whitehouse travelled the country in search of candidates sympathetic to her views on video nasties:

'One of the marginals we went to was Luton which was Mr Graham Bright's seat. I think he'd only got in the previous election by several hundred votes. Now we met him and the local paper came along. We asked him about the video nasties and he was very supportive to what we were doing. All this was in the local paper. He got in again with a majority, I think, of 6000 or something like that. Then when the draw for the private Members' ballot was made at the very beginning of the new session of Parliament, who should be the first one to draw his name out but Graham Bright. So he used his opportunity to introduce a private Member's bill to control video nasties.'

The League Against Cruel Sports has been less successful with private Members' bills. In *The Politics of Hunting* (1983) Richard Thomas recalls that when private Members' time was re-introduced after the war in 1948, Arthur Greenwood persuaded the MP at the top of the private Members' ballot, Mr Cocks from Broxtowe, to introduce an anti-stag hunting and coursing bill. Nothing came of it. Between 1967 and 1977, 16 private Members' bills on the subject failed, even though Harold Wilson's Labour Government made parliamentary time available for debate on hare coursing. Despite such support, a private Member's bill has little chance of success against strong opposition, unless the Government is prepared to take it up. With anti-hunting legislation the main barrier is the House of Lords. Kevin McNamara's bill to abolish hare coursing had a majority of 117 in the Commons but failed to get through the Lords, despite receiving the support of the Wilson Government (although that Government was not in a strong position having a majority of only four). This failure is mainly due to the parliamentary tactics employed by the supporters and sympathisers of the British Field Sports Society who oppose anti-hunting legislation. They talked out a bill on the subject in 1972 by intervening continuously and at length during preceding business. This meant that debating time ran out before it could even come up for discussion.

In 1957 the same technique was used by pro-hanging MPs to talk out Sidney Silverman's private Member's bill to abolish capital punishment. In *Capital Punishment and British Politics* (1962), J. B. Cristoph describes what happened:

> 'On February 1st, a private Members' day in the House of Commons, a small band of Conservative Members made what to the innocent observer seemed to be a series of harmless speeches about an innocuous hire purchases bill. They were actually administering the *coup de grâce* to the Silverman abolition bill. By arranging for a full roster of Conservative speakers on the first of the two private Members' bills scheduled to debate that Friday, the rententionists managed to use up the entire five hours allotted for both bills ... Despite abolitionist entreaties against the filibuster, the Speaker refused to halt a customary procedure of the House, and the faint hope that somehow Members would have a chance to vote once again on a straight abolition bill expired, victim of a series of successful government strategems.'

The pro-abortion lobby were also to use parliamentary procedure to obstruct the passage of John Corrie's private Member's bill to amend the 1967 Abortion Act. Marsh and Chambers in *Pressure Politics: Interest Groups in Britain* (Marsh ed., 1983) believe that the abortion lobby learnt from their experience with the William Benyon bill in 1975 that they had insufficient knowledge of parliamentary procedure. So when the Corrie bill was passing through its stages in the 1979/80 parliamentary session, they enlisted the help of Ian Mikardo and Willie Hamilton, two experienced parliamentarians with extensive knowledge of procedural tactics.

One tactic was to postpone the introduction of amendments until the Report Stage, rather then introduce them at the Committee Stage, and thus ensure that the Speaker would have to call those proposing them to speak at the Report Stage. This related to their second tactic which was to exploit the time limit on debate at the Report Stage. Eighty amendments were tabled for consideration at the Report Stage. The Speaker selected 50 which referred to 28 sections of the bill, each of which had to be debated and voted on separately. Only by dropping a large part of their bill could its sponsors have ensured its passage. In the debate, the pro-abortionists, Marsh and Chambers recall, were: 'anxious not to be accused of filibustering, [so they] organised numerous speakers who were willing to make short but frequent speeches; the longest any MP spoke for on this side was half as hour.' The obstructionist tactics succeeded and Corrie's bill never reached the statute books.

3.3   *Hiring help*

Information concerning what's happening in Parliament and how to establish contacts with MPs can be obtained by the use of a specialist public relations company. There are about 30 companies which offer services for those who are able to afford the price. Evie Soames, who is joint Managing Director with Arthur Butler of Charles Barker Watney and Powell Ltd, describes the likely cost to the client:

> 'It varies, depending on what a particular client wishes to be done or how much the information would cost. A large manufacturing company like Unilever would obviously need a greater intensity of information and monitoring than a smaller company which is only interested in one particular area. There are not many people we take on for less than £1500. Sometimes we charge between £1500 and £10 000 or maybe more.'

Professional lobby firms, described as 'Parliamentary Consultants' in *Hollis*, the Press and Public Relations Annual, are not new but there has been a sudden upsurge in numbers in the last few years with many being formed by MPs in the current Parliament. Michael Forsyth, Conservative MP for Stirling since the 1983 General Election is director of Michael Forsyth Associates Ltd. Political Research & Communication International (PR & CI) has Peter Fry, the Conservative MP for Wellingborough, as its Chairman. The longest established is Watney and Powell, which started in the 1920s. It was taken over by Charles Barker in 1974.

There are two distinct functions which a public relations company can offer. Firstly, it can provide an information service monitoring all the information sources, both written and oral. The main sources are written and include all the government and parliamentary publications like green papers, white papers, select committee reports, *Hansard*, parliamentary order papers, statutory instruments, departmental reports, government press releases etc. This involves the labour-intensive process of going through all the paperwork, cutting out relevant sections and sending them to clients.

The second function is liaison and lobbying for clients. This involves finding out which MPs and ministers have a personal, ideological, or constituency interest relating to that of the client organisation whether it be a company, charity or campaigning organisation. Spotting the right people to contact is the first step to arranging meetings between client and politician, sometimes over lunch or on a short, expenses-paid trip. Contact is not only maintained with politicians but also with relevant civil servants and pressmen.

In its efforts to 'Save the GLC' the Greater London Council hired an independent parliamentary consultancy firm, Roland Freeman Ltd. Roland Freeman is now an SDP supporter but had previously been a Conservative candidate in the 1974 General Election. A current Conservative Party supporter, Francis Sitwell, was hired to work on the campaign to brief Conservative MPs and peers and to organise meetings. Ken Livingstone explains another aspect of the campaign:

'We've built up a series of contacts and knowledge about where we should concentrate our efforts. A body of data is being built up about the particular interests of leading members of each of the parties. We have a computer index system so that we know which SDP members are mainly interested in the arts and recreation. We get to them and tell them what will happen if the GLC is abolished. We know who are interested in industry and employment and in race relations. There is no good going to somebody who is obsessed about industry and employment and talking about the quality of the arts and recreation.'

A number of MPs operate directly as consultants and are hired directly by companies. Martin Stevens, Conservative MP for Fulham, is hired by Woolworths, others are hired by interest groups. Eldon Griffith, Conservative MP for Bury St Edmunds, is paid by the Police Federation. Because of their financial link with these lobby groups, MPs are expected to declare this interest in the Register of Members' Interests, which was introduced in the 1974–9 Parliament. Despite initial difficulties (Enoch Powell, for instance, refused to co-operate), the Register was published in both the 1979 Parliament and the 1983 Parliament. One of the reasons for setting up the Register was to ensure that payments from companies to MPs, as well as any other financial interests such as sponsorship by a trade union, ownership of shares, property and professional earnings, were brought out into the open to counter accusations of impropriety.

In 1984 a parliamentary select committee, as a result of the growth in the numbers involved and the level of activity, is examining the proposal that public relations firms should be registered and have to make an annual report on their parliamentary work, just as professional lobbyists are and do in Washington.

Financial inducements to MPs to sustain an interest in a company's business is not a new phenomenon, but recently it has become more organised, more professional and more obvious. Nineteenth-century railway companies would automatically take MPs and peers onto the Board of Directors. Certain engineering companies established a tradition of having a Conservative MP on the Board of Directors.

There are two problems in all this. The first is to identify whose interest the MP represents. The second is the possibility of corruption. Both might be resolved if financial considerations were openly recorded and then registered for inspection so that constituents at election time would know if a candidate is also paid to represent a business, a trade union, a charity, a profession, or a campaign group. After all, constituents already know that MPs have a prior loyalty to their political party and they may not think the two loyalties irreconcilable or even that it is desirable to separate the 'paid' interest from constituency concerns.

But the current practice as far as the Register of Members' Interests is concerned is not rigorous enough, mainly because the MP records in it only what he chooses to. A more independent assessment is necessary than currently exists. Furthermore, Andrew Roth thinks that the registrars are not assertive enough in getting MPs to fill in their returns for the Register under the present system:

'I don't think the registrars are tough enough. They don't even go to the point of educating MPs as to what they're supposed to do. For example, I had a lot of fun with Cyril Smith some time back because [he] announced in the Register that he had a shareholding in Turner and Newell. Now Turner and Newell is the big asbestos factory in his constituency of Rochdale and of course it's been under fire from various sources because of the whole problem from the danger of asbestos, and Cyril was showing his identification with the problems of the company. But so far as the Register is concerned, you're only supposed to register shareholdings when you have four per cent of the company's shares and this, since the company is a forty million pounds company, would make Cyril a millionaire. So I did a story on this and I congratulated Cyril on being a millionaire. He said: "What do you mean?" I said: "Well, you said you have a shareholding in Turner and Newell which means it must be at least four per cent that you've got, and as it's a forty million pounds company so therefore you're a millionaire by definition." "I never knew that", he said. But he didn't register his own company of which he owned 32 per cent.'

The current proposal being discussed in Parliament is the idea of setting up a register of professional lobby companies as exists in the USA. Statutory registration and regulation was introduced there in 1946 following a number of corruption scandals. One of the points which will require clarification is not only whether the MP should register a financial interest, but whether members of their immediate family should also be included. Mark Thatcher's and Denis Thatcher's business interests have led some MPs to demand more scrutiny of the entire family's business interests. Margaret Thatcher's view is that it is a private matter not requiring disclosure.

Apart from the constitutional issue of whose interest is being represented by MPs, there is the further question of possible financial corruption. Parliamentarians are concerned to prevent the recurrence of a scandal such as that which involved the Newcastle architect John Poulson, who received a seven-year prison sentence in 1974 for corruption.

By presenting them with gifts and free holidays, Poulson had systematically corrupted official and elected representatives in his pursuit of local and central government contracts. When the scandal broke, only one of the MPs who had received money from Poulson – John Cordle – resigned his seat. Others, like Reggie Maudling and Albert Roberts, did not. Geoffrey Alderman, academic writer on politics, points out:

'The anomaly that the Poulson affair and its aftermath brought home to us was that a civil servant, or for that matter a local government officer, can be charged with a criminal offence under the Prevention of Corruption Act and indeed can be imprisoned for acting corruptly by accepting bribes. But a Member of Parliament cannot. The late Reginald Maudling was not prosecuted. I really don't see why an MP who accepts a bribe or acts corruptly should not go to prison just like a local government officer or civil servant.'

Andrew Roth gives one explanation of how Reginald Maudling became involved:

'I think Maudling was corrupted by pressures on him. He had a peculiar attitude towards money matters. I think he was largely careless. He was a lovely man in very many ways. He was a very decent, attractive and approachable man, but there were a lot of pressures on him including pressures from his family who wanted to live well, enjoy the good things of life. If you are not a very well endowed Conservative MP and a Cabinet minister and you see around you very well endowed Conservative MPs and Cabinet ministers who've inherited wealth, there is a certain temptation to get on the gravy train . . . He had one or two people very close to him who are blamed by Conservatives for having pushed too many opportunities his way.'

3.4   *Ideology*

An important consideration for lobbyists to bear in mind is the ideology of the governing party. Success can often depend on couching proposals in terms which include catch-phrases likely to appeal to certain ideological outlooks. David Tench, the Consumers' Association's legal adviser, paid particular attention to this aspect when drafting the House Buyers Bill, by using terms which he knew would appeal to the *laissez-faire* outlook of the current Conservative Government. He told the press:

> 'A blast or, failing that, a whiff of competition from outside the legal profession is needed to blow away the cobwebs that bedevil the business of buying houses.'

Here he explains why he used this particular phrasing:

> '... this Government's policy is very much centred on competition. Competition is the answer to the evils of society, at least certainly the consumer ones. Here was a new Government with a new intake of new boys, all zealously accepting competition as the key to political philosophy. So we, as it were, dressed up the reform of the house transfer system as being essentially a matter of competition. We actually believe that as well, but it's a question of emphasis, and of highlighting it. Now if we had a Labour Government in power I think our approach would be totally different, it would have essentially been a matter of protecting the citizen, giving better rights, a better deal to the ordinary individual by virtue of consumer protection.'

The desire to promote the ideology and practice of greater competition had already led to the 1981 Forestry Act which enabled the Government to dispose of Forestry Commission land partly to provide income and partly to encourage the steady flow of land out of public into private and commercial hands. Patrick Cormack, Conservative MP, believed that the ideological concern with 'incentives to efficiency' encouraged a larger amount of Forestry Commission land to be sold off than otherwise would have been the case.

To many people's surprise, the Government committed to the ideological pursuit of 'greater competition as a spur to efficiency' turned its attention not only to the nationalised industries and quasi-government agencies like the Arts Council and the Forestry Commission, but also to the professions. Solicitors and opticians were to be targets of government proposals for reforms of their professional practice. The opticians were a surprising example as they had received no 'bad press' in the way that the solicitors had. But their monopoly in supplying spectacles nevertheless became the target of a government attack. Andrew Roth believes this to have been essentially for doctrinal reasons and explains the opticians' response:

'For what looks like purely doctrinal reasons [the opticians] came in for government scrutiny – an influence of the Institute of Economic Affairs and the Adam Smith Institute, which had affected Mrs Thatcher's thinking and the thinking of a few other members of her Government, like Sir Keith Joseph. They developed as part of their theology the idea that you should break the monopoly of the professions. The opticians certainly were caught by surprise and they reacted rather belatedly. They took on professional consultants who began to brief MPs and this was one of the examples where this sort of belated resistance showed up in the debate, which took place in May 1984 in the Commons.

The Health Minister, Kenneth Clarke, was very much alone and there were a whole lot of MPs who were attacking him from various parts of the House including his own side. One had the feeling that Kenneth Clarke himself was not all that enthusiastic about the new legislation because his heart didn't seem to be in it. This answers the question of whether it's worth fighting in the House. The opticians briefed quite a number of MPs with the help of a PR company. Of course Jill Knight, whose husband is an optician, was right in the thick of things telling them what a wonderful job people like her husband did for society.'

What is unusual about the current Government's attachment to ideology is that in the past Conservative Governments have prided themselves upon their pragmatism and chided their socialist opponents for their commitment to doctrine. But the Conservative Government from 1979 onwards has unashamedly adopted the *laissez-faire* rhetoric of competition and 'rolling back the State', as well as the general monetarist view and commitment to 'free market forces' as espoused and outlined by the Institute of Economic Affairs and the Adam Smith Institute. In the past this would have been unthinkable. Andrew Roth had long had the feeling that when you started discussing theory with Conservatives, 'they almost took out a horse whip'.

Ideology is not just a set of ideas which exist in a social vacuum. It represents the beliefs of those whose interests are best served when and if those beliefs are translated into practice. Roth's view of ideology is similar to the Marxist attitude to the relationship between ideas and interest but he does not adopt a crude theory that ideas are simply and automatically a reflection of self-interest. Ideology can be an autonomous influence on political events. Andrew Roth:

> 'I do not see ideology as a disembodied aspect of society because it serves the interest of those people who are pushing it. But ideology can be influential within its own right. The pure ideology of monetarism as found in Adam Smith does exist totally in its own right as a survival of an earlier ideology. But it is also part of the general ideology of capitalism. Now there's no direct one-to-one relationship between ideologies and their economic base. It doesn't mean if you are the owner of a big factory you automatically become a monetarist or believe in Adam Smith. As a matter of fact most industrialists develop a rather pragmatic approach to how they run their factories.'

3.5   *The Consumers' Association versus the Law Society*

In Chapter 1, Michael Young described the early days of the Consumers' Association and its origins in a Bethnal Green garage. By 1961, its membership had reached a quarter of a million people and new offices were found in a more fashionable area just off the Strand in Buckingham Street. In 1971, it achieved its first lobbying success with the passing of the Unsolicited Goods and Services Act, and in 1972 Geoffrey Howe was appointed as the first ever Minister for Consumer Affairs. The Association's rise in effectiveness continued and later legislative successes included the 1974 Consumer Credit Act introduced by Geoffrey Howe, the Fair Trading

Act of 1973, and the 1977 Unfair Contract Terms Act. With the British membership of the EEC in 1973 the Association set its sights on the Common Market Commission, and by 1981 a Directorate-General for Environmental and Consumer Protection had been established.

Its most recent success has been its attack on the solicitors' monopoly on conveyancing through Austin Mitchell's private Member's bill. David Tench, the Association's legal adviser explained earlier in this chapter how this came about and pinpointed the advantages of a lobby group being well prepared and able to act speedily once the ballot for private Members' bills has been made.

Of the occupational groups who have felt their job-security threatened by the Government in recent years (and these include coal miners and opticians), no group could have been more surprised about it than the solicitors. In Parliament, local government, Whitehall and the Conservative Party solicitors are well represented. A conservative profession, dealing to a large extent with matters of contract and property, must have felt secure when the Conservatives took office under Margaret Thatcher in 1979. However, the parliamentary session of 1983/4, which coincided with the period when Christopher Hewetson – now Sir Christopher – took over the office of President of the Law Society, quickly dispelled any complacency.

The Law Society of England and Wales was founded in 1825. It has a very splendid building in Chancery Lane and is organised on the basis of 122 local Law Societies who send representatives to the Council of the Law Society. Of the 44 000 practising solicitors in England and Wales, 38 000 are members of the Law Society. The Law Society is a good illustration of the sort of advantages that interest groups can acquire in terms of resources. Not only can it afford a palatial reading room, library and dining room, but it can also provide the salaries of 1550 full-time staff, of whom 1225 are employed to administer the Legal Aid scheme – the deputy Secretary-General of the Law Society is also the Secretary of Legal Aid.

Even among solicitors disputes about the way the Law Society should be organised had persisted for some time. A radical minority wanted annual elections for the Council which controls the Society, instead of the system whereby local solicitors delegated representatives. A further row concerned the system of collective insurance against negligence, the solicitors' indemnity scheme which is run by the Law Society. It was claimed that the system of contributions into the scheme benefited the larger, urban and more influential firms in the profession at the expense of the smaller, rural solicitor.

To this was added the inability of the Law Society to keep out of the headlines. One headline-achieving story involved an ex-member of the Law Society Council, Mr Glanville Davies, who overcharged Mr Leslie Parsons, a South Wales business man, by £131 000. Such instances led to the demand that solicitors should introduce an independent complaints procedure rather than continue the existing system whereby solicitors investigate complaints against each other.

Ole Hansen, director of the Legal Action Group, a radical organisation within the profession established in 1971, comments on these problems:

> 'An enormous amount of publicity was generated when the Law Society failed to act for a period of seven years in respect of a case of gross misconduct on the part of a Council member. This has perhaps received most attention. An example of a conflict of interest between public good and professional interest which comes up now and again stems from the fact that the Law Society, as well as being a trade union, is also the body that runs the Legal Aid scheme. It is part of public administration in that sense. It's rather as if the British Medical Association, which is a registered trade union, unlike the Law Society, was running the National Health Service.'

Many of the criticisms of the legal profession had been discussed in the Royal Commission on the Provision of Legal Services, chaired by an accountant, Sir Henry Benson, which finished its work in 1979. Despite nearly 300 recommendations, radical critics of the legal profession were disappointed to find that on all the controversial issues the *status quo* prevailed.

Perhaps the profession had been lulled into a false sense of security by the Royal Commission's tacit approval of many of its traditional practices. As it was, Christopher Hewetson must have thought he had more than enough problems to spoil his one year of glory as President. But in the July of 1983 an unpredicted attack was launched on the solicitors' monopoly on conveyancing. David Tench of the Consumers' Association who put up the idea; Austin Mitchell, the backbench Labour MP who drew a high place in the ballot for introducing a private Member's bill; the Thatcher Government, which encouraged the otherwise speculative proposal and indicated support – these were the demons who must have given Christopher Hewetson nightmares. Not unexpectedly he blamed the media for ruining his year in office. Just after the second reading of the House Buyers Bill, he wrote a letter to all solicitors' firms suggesting that the solicitors' case had been misrepresented by a hostile press.

Austin Mitchell did not reveal the contents of the bill until the last moment in order to make it more difficult to prepare a case against it. So how did the Law Society respond to this unexpected attack on its monopoly on house conveyancing? (Unexpected in that the Benson Committee only five years earlier had recommended the retention of that monopoly on the grounds that it was the single most important financial source for the profession? To undermine it would threaten the livelihoods of many solicitors.) Sir Christopher Hewetson:

'We have in each local Law Society a parliamentary liaison officer and he gets in touch with his local MPs to try and keep them in the picture about our side, and I think we like to try and establish good relations between local solicitors and local MPs because we can in fact help them with their surgeries, as they have constituents coming in with problems which are quite often legal problems.

Well, we hadn't had a campaign of this sort involving a parliamentary bill for some time and I felt we were not experts here and that we should get expert advice. So we brought in a firm to advise us as to how we should go about making our contacts and how our staff members, who were involved in parliamentary relations, should go around lobbying MPs and we got a lot of valuable advice on that.'

The Law Society brought in to help them a company they had worked with before, the public relations firm of Charles Barker, Watney and Powell. In the meantime the mood of public, Parliament and Government was crystallising.

In July 1983 the bill was put into the Table Office of the House of Commons by 5.00 p.m. on the last day for submitting private Members' bills. The long title of the bill was: 'A Bill to Improve Competition in Relation to House Transfer Services'.

The Consumers' Association had never accepted the Benson recommendation concerning the retention of the conveyancing monopoly. David Tench explains his feeling about the issue when the bill was introduced:

> 'I thought this was a very big issue and a difficult one with a very vigorous opponent, the Law Society, representing solicitors. I thought that this probably would take about five years to really get through and that this was the first step in getting it discussed in Parliament. It would not succeed, of course, but we would make a little progress with coverage in the media and it would be a marker on a long and stony road. So I wrongly forecast the way it went, because within two or three months this issue had taken off in the most amazing way. It was taken up by the media so that, for example, we had editorial support from every one of the national newspapers. I think partly our success was due to the fact it was very badly handled by the Law Society who opposed it most vigorously and vituperatively. They misjudged the mood of Parliament, of the media and of the nation as a whole.
>
> The success of that bill demonstrates another aspect which is that when you're a lobby group you've got to pick up the mood of the times. There are many consumer issues around that we might have chosen at that time but we didn't. We said that this was a bill about competition which at that time was to the forefront of government policy.'

By choosing a topic and presenting it in a way which was consistent with current government philosophy, the Consumers' Association had ensured that the Government was at least initially neutral. Otherwise it could have destroyed the bill's chances through its ability to control the business, and in particular the timetable of business, in the House of Commons. The bill had a second reading in December 1983; it only just survived, receiving 100 votes – the bare minimum required. This unexpected success galvanised the whole campaign and for the first time it became apparent that there was enough parliamentary, press and public support to achieve success. More importantly, the Government moved from a position of neutrality to one of cautious support. David Tench:

> 'The Government was minded to do something. The bill had announced rather half-baked proposals about re-forming the house transfer system. That was in the expectation that the bill would be lost, but when the bill was passed at its second reading, the Government attitude changed very markedly ... we spent about two months negotiating with the Government about what they might do to take on the main issues raised by the bill. Finally, in the following February, a government policy was hammered out and the Government came forward with very positive and exciting proposals. This was a big issue that couldn't really go through as a private Member's bill. But it demonstrated the value of a private Member's bill by raising a major issue and getting it in front of the public and in front of Parliament.'

A meeting was set up on 15 November 1983 between the press officers and the parliamentary liaison officers of the 122 local Law Societies to discuss tactics. Minutes were taken and circulated. They talked of putting 'pressure' on MPs and making efforts to ensure hostile MPs were kept away from the House at the time of the debate. These minutes got into the hands of the press, which led MPs to refer the matter to the Speaker as a possible breach of parliamentary privilege. In the event, the speaker did not consider it to be a breach of parliamentary privilege, although it did indicate clumsy counter-lobbying.

Sir Christopher Hewetson denies that anything 'improper' was discussed at the meeting:

> 'At the meeting were the parliamentary liaison officers from local Law Societies who we were briefing on the

particular points that we wished to get over in our campaign. I suppose we obviously discussed how the particular debate would go in the House on the second reading. But certainly there was never any intention that any improper pressure should be put on MPs in any way at all. Put simply, we weren't going to encourage them to go if they were known to be in favour of the bill.

A minute of this private meeting was circulated confidentially to the people who were at that meeting. I think the particular point that was made in that meeting was probably a jocular reference which in fact came out in cold print in a slightly different form. Nevertheless, having got into the hands of Austin Mitchell and his supporters, it's not surprising they made the maximum propaganda use of it.'

The Law Society's opponents cashed in on the publicity by pointing to the desperation of the Law Society's tactics. Even MPs who were unlikely to threaten the traditional legal profession's cosy relationship with the Conservative Party were upset by what they considered to be the heavy-handed nature of its reaction to the bill. Julian Critchley comments:

'They were foolish to overstate their case and to threaten, albeit indirectly, the integrity of Members, because what really gets our backs up and makes us even stuffier and more pompous than we usually are is any perceived challenge to what we consider to be our integrity or our freedom.'

David Tench was surprised by the degree of personal attack on him and Austin Mitchell:

'I think they went to the professional lobby too late. I wouldn't criticise the professional lobbyist – it was the utterances of the people in the Law Society themselves. They very much personalised the campaign as if Mr Austin Mitchell and myself were lunatics and had some personal spite against the Law Society.'

Andrew Roth gives this assessment of the Law Society's tactics:

'Of course the Law Society acted very stupidly by passing on to every solicitor [the tactics discussed at the November meeting. It had been suggested that it] might be a good idea for solicitors to arrange an appointment for MPs who were hostile so as to keep them out of the House of Commons on that Friday. The Law Society sent this out in a form which was immediately leaked and was seen to be one of dirty politics and a breach of privilege. They telegraphed all their punches, as you say in boxing . . . The solicitors of course would have been very well advised to have just said, "There are very few conveyancers who are threatening us. Of course we will help train them so they don't make any mistakes and we will help the conveyancers' organisers to set up an institute and examination system; and work on the basis that we might lose three, four or five, even 10, maybe 15 per cent of our business over a period of time." Instead they attacked the proposals and they didn't fully realise the amount of hostility there was to solicitors for overcharging in this and other fields. Everybody was astonished, including myself, by the fact they lost out in the Austin Mitchell bill.'

The final comment comes from Sir Christopher Hewetson:

'Well, of course you can always see afterwards that perhaps our opposition came over too stridently.'

3.6   *When influencing Parliament matters*

For much of the time parliamentary business is controlled by the Government in spite of the constitutional textbooks' rhetoric about the 'sovereignty of Parliament'. As we have seen, the House Buyers Bill only had a chance of being enacted if the Government were prepared to support it. It might therefore seem clear that lobbying activity is more effective if it focuses its efforts on convincing the Government of the day of the merits of the proposals it supports rather than Parliament.

But there are times when matters are not so simple – as, for example, when there is a general election. Our system of parliamentary government requires the executive to be able to command the support of Parliament. Hence, lobbying the candidates can be of use at election time because a lobby group might thereby help to influence the outcome of the election so that a Government which has some sympathy with their interests or cause is elected. Furthermore, candidates are often more open to receive and listen to emissaries from lobby organisations during the uncertain days before they actually reach Parliament. Mary Whitehouse was able to nobble John Corrie in this way. She toured 20 marginal constituencies during the 1983 General Election campaign in a van from which she spoke to groups of people in town centres carrying the NVALA slogan to the electorate and endorsing the candidate who would 'fight for decency'. She found this an 'incredible experience':

> 'I didn't support any particular candidate. In any case this was during the election so we would not have taken a political side. We had a caravan and I came out of a hole in the top of this caravan ... I had a microphone and each place that we went to we let the local papers and the local MP know in advance that we were coming. And in every case the press came to meet us outside the city and would sit in the caravan and see what was happening. When we got into a crowded place I'd come out through the top. I'd never done anything like that in my life before.'

Frank Field found that he had to combat the activities of SPUC (the Society for the Protection of the Unborn Child) as the sitting MP in his strongly Catholic Merseyside seat of Birkenhead:

> 'On Friday, before the last Thursday of polling day, the clergy in Birkenhead received a letter saying, "This is the record of your Member; you ought to know this and you can of course use this in church on Sunday if you wish". Had they done so I would have had no right of reply because that was the last Sunday before votes were cast. One of the Catholic clergy, who I don't think is a natural supporter of mine, made contact and therefore I was able to get a letter out. As I understand it no priest used the SPUC information on the Sunday before polling day.'

Identifying candidates sympathetic to a lobby is carried out much more comprehensively at election time in the USA when computer lists of past congressional voting performance are sent to lobby supporters in an attempt to sway their voting intentions. This tactic is less developed in the UK, but as the Mary Whitehouse and Frank Field stories reveal, it does occur on a less grand scale.

Apart from during the election period there are two other situations when Parliamentarians do have influence and hence became worthy of the lobbyists' concentrated effort. One is when there is no clear majority and MPs can find themselves in a strong bargaining position with the government whips, as happened with the Labour Government in the Parliament of 1974–79. Frank Field MP, previously Director of CPAG, describes the 'gift of events' during a period when the Labour Government had the narrowest of majorities which helped to benefit the CPAG's campaign for child benefits:

'My tenure at Child Poverty Action Group covered a period when the group was enormously lucky in that we had a major leak of Cabinet papers and at the end of the period the Government in the House of Commons didn't have a majority. It was a combination of those two: the leak about how the Labour Government was retracting promises on fully implementing a child-benefit scheme; and the Government not being able to control the House of Commons. One could work away, building up coalitions without formally telling people they were part of a coalition. The Tribunite Labour MPs were pushing very firmly on this commitment, as was Patrick Jenkin from the Tories ... In that situation the Government found it very difficult in the final analysis to control its budget. It made a major concession ... This gift of events coming together gave the campaign for child benefit a major leap forward and resulted in an extra one and a half billion a year going into the purses of mothers.'

The other occasion when MPs are worth lobbying directly is when a free vote is given on an issue, free that is of party whips and voting guidelines. Free votes are held on issues where there is no laid-down party line, such as capital punishment, abortion and the wearing of safety belts in cars. The usually quoted reason for permitting such votes is that the issue is a moral one, and MPs are divided on both sides of the House on the issue.

Cynics make the point that free votes are a means of the Government avoiding the political embarrassment of being associated with legislation which is potentially unpopular or controversial. Certainly the question of capital punishment is one where Governments have consistently allowed a free vote rather than incur any public wrath. Pro-abortionists have consequently tended to concentrate their lobbying efforts on persuading MPs rather than trying to convert public opinion.

'In the past', wrote J. B. Christoph in *Capital Punishment and British Politics* (1962) of the period leading up to 1947, 'all bills concerned with the question of capital punishment had been put to free votes on some or all of their stages.' In 1947 the Home Secretary, Chuter-Ede, was faced with a backbench revolt amongst the swollen ranks of Labour MPs in the 1945–50 Parliament, because the Criminal Justice Bill, introduced in that year, did not include any reference to abolishing hanging as the Attlee Cabinet thought this might jeopardise the chance of getting through a number of other reforms in penal policy. In 1948, during the passage of the bill, MPs voted to add an amending clause abolishing capital punishment, only to have the House of Lords vote to retain the death penalty. To play for time the Government promised to set up a Royal Commission on the death penalty – a classic example of procrastination – and dropped the abolition amendment from the Criminal Justice Bill which then became law in 1948.

The Royal Commission on Capital Punishment was established in 1949, but did not produce its report until 1953 by which time the Conservatives had replaced Labour as the party of government. The subsequent demand for a parliamentary debate on the Royal Commission's findings was reluctantly granted. This took place in 1955 and the free vote again led to a majority of MPs supporting abolition but the Lords once again voting against. However, this period of parliamentary interest did generate a sense of confidence amongst the abolition lobby as twice since the war only the House of Lords had prevented the end of hanging. The Howard League – which was the lobby group concerned – renewed its efforts, helped by a new group formed by Canon John Collins, Victor Gollancz and Arthur Koestler, which called itself the National Campaign for the Abolition of the

Death Penalty. A further free vote came in 1956 with Sidney Silverman's private Member's bill. Again a majority of MPs were in favour but the Lords opposed it. Then the bill was overtaken by the Homicide Act of 1957 which brought in the new category of non-capital murders.

With the return of the Labour Party to Government in 1964, Sidney Silverman was encouraged by the Government to introduce a new bill. This time both the Commons and Lords were in accord and so the Murder (Abolition of the Death Penalty) Act was passed after a free vote in 1965. Initially abolition was for a trial period only. Then in a free vote in 1969 Parliament decided to abolish capital punishment for murder for an indefinite period. In 1975 and 1983 motions to restore hanging were defeated by large majorities in the Commons, again after free votes.

The part played by the Lords in this story of capital punishment lobbying is an apt reminder that there are two Houses of Parliament, and a number of lobby groups have been able to find helpful allies amongst the peers. A large majority in the House of Commons on the Government's side has existed since 1979, but the House of Lords have managed to defeat the Government on a record number of occasions, helped by the 209 crossbenchers who don't take a party whip.

Mike Daube, speaking of the ASH campaign, comments:

'I think people often forget just how useful the House of Lords can be. In terms of political clout it doesn't really matter very much, but it's a place to get problems aired. It's a place for publicity, it's a place where the Government has to answer questions, and it is a place where you can get as much time as you like, whereas in the Commons time is very severely rationed. I used it quite a bit for questions, for mini-debates and just to get a bit of pressure put on the Government. The House of Lords is a good place to get things going and I was very lucky that there were some very good medical peers and other peers who were prepared to play ball.'

In addition, there are many life peers who have been successful in a range of professional, business and political careers. And one consequence of having hereditary peers is that they are not answerable to anyone – the only Communist views in Parliament are to be heard in the Lords – and this makes for greater independence than is found in the Commons. However, the House of Lords is only secondary in potential power to the House of Commons and both are subject to the power of the Government and, in particular, the Prime Minister. Des Wilson sees Margaret Thatcher's Government as an extreme in prime ministerial government.

'The key thing with the Lords is that they're much more independent-minded generally, they're not frightened of the Prime Minister, and therefore you can get much more all-party action in the Lords and you can get very distinguished people with a lot of experience who will identify with a campaign ... [but] at the end of the day the thing is going to have to go to the Commons and the real power-house is the Commons.

I don't think many people would argue that we have reached the extreme in prime ministerial government at the moment. This Government is run by Mrs Thatcher. It's not always been the case. Harold Wilson in his last years used to talk about being the centre-forward in the team and undoubtedly the individual members had a great deal of discretion at that time. At the moment Mrs Thatcher is running the show. If she happens to agree with you that's marvellous. If she doesn't, you're in real trouble. She agreed with CLEAR (the Campaign for Lead Free Air) – and that was a factor, but she does not agree with the Campaign for Freedom of Information. At the moment the House of Commons is important because that's where the vote takes place, that's where the big debates take place, and that's the one place where you can corner a minister who has ultimately to answer to the house.'

Lord Young of Dartington, originator of the Consumers' Association, the Open University, the SSRC and the National Extension College. He possesses an amazing ability to translate ideas into successful institutions, yet has a low media profile. 'Success depends' he says, 'not on having a larger-than-life personality, but on persistence and having a good central idea, whose time has come.'

Des Wilson – high profile and many successes. His personal story reads like a history of post-1960s lobby groups. He has been associated with Shelter, CPAG, NCCL, CLEAR, *Friends of the Earth and the 1984 Freedom of Information Campaign.*

Ken Livingstone, Labour Party member, at a fringe meeting of the 1984 Tory Party Conference, lobbying for the retention of the GLC.

Sir Charles Cunningham, Permanent Secretary at the Home Office from 1957–66. Since 1900 there have been 33 Home Secretaries and only 12 Permanent Secretaries. Their continuity is the basis of their influence.

The Arts in danger

THE ARTS IN DANGER

We the undersigned view with the gravest alarm the Government's proposals for the arts in the event of the abolition of the Greater London Council and the Metropolitan County Councils. These proposals list only 16 bodies whose survival appears to be of some concern to the Government; 6 museums, 3 orchestras and the London Orchestral Concert Board, 2 theatres, 2 opera companies, 1 ballet company, and the South Bank Arts complex in London. Nine are based in London and seven outside it. However, even in these cases, no promise is made that present levels of funding by local government will be maintained.

For the many hundreds of other arts bodies, of all sizes, supported by the GLC and the Metropolitan County Councils there is no comfort. They must look to borough and district councils for their future support.

For decades the general pattern of support for the arts from borough and district councils has been unpredictable, and in some cases hopelessly inadequate. With today's constraints on local government expenditure it is doubtful if such councils will be able to replace the money for the arts which the Government now intends to remove from the GLC and the Metropolitan County Councils.

The Government's proposals constitute an unprecedented attack upon the arts which will diminish the quality of life in this country, and with it our claim to be accounted a civilised society.

We call upon the Government to reassure the thousands of artists in this country, and the millions who constitute their audiences, that it will not cause any further reduction in the already inadequate funding of the arts in Britain.

PAT ABRAHAM • MARIA AITKEN • JOHN ALDERTON • BRIAN ALDISS • LINDSAY ANDERSON • HARRY ANDREWS • ALAN AYCKBOURN • ROBIN BAILEY • DAME JANET BAKER • TOM BAKER • JOAN BAKEWELL • PETER BARKWORTH • CLIVE BARNES • ALAN BATES • QUENTIN BELL • JILL BENNETT • LORD BERNSTEIN • MICHAEL BLAKEMORE • ROBERT BOLT • PETER BOWLES • LORD BRABOURNE • MALCOLM BRADBURY • MELVYN BRAGG • RICHARD BRIERS • ELEANOR BRON • BRIGID BROPHY

PETER BROOK • MICHAEL BRYANT • VINCENT BURKE • HUMPHREY BURTON • JAMES CAMERON • SIR HUGH CASSON • JULIE CHRISTIE • MICHAEL CODRON • GEORGE COLE • JILLY COOPER • HUNTER DAVIES • SIR COLIN DAVIS • JOHN DEXTER • JONATHAN DIMBLEBY • CHRISTOPHER DUNKLEY • PAUL EDDINGTON • HAROLD EVANS • SIR ROGER FALK • FRANK FINLAY • ALBERT FINNEY • SUSAN FLEETWOOD • BRUCE FORSYTHE • JOHN FOWLES • MICHAEL FRAYN • SIR JOHN GIELGUD • PETER GILL

JACK GOLD • SIR CHARLES GROVES • SIR PETER HALL • SUSAN HAMPSHIRE • CHRISTOPHER HAMPTON • ROBERT HARDY • DAVID HARE • ALASTAIR HETHERINGTON • SAM HASKINS • RICHARD HOGGART • TOM HOPKINSON • SIR TOM HOPKINSON • AIR MICHAEL HORDERN • JOHN HURT • DEREK JACOBI • GEMMA JONES • MIRIAM KARLIN

LUDOVIC KENNEDY • VICTORIA LAMONT • VERITY LAMBERT • DINSDALE LANDEN • DORIS LESSING • JOSEPH LOSEY • BILL McALISTER • ROGER McGOUGH • ARTHUR MARSHALL • FRANCIS MATTHEWS • GEORGE MELLY • LORD MILES • WARREN MITCHELL • HENRY MOORE • ERIC MORECAMBE • SHERIDAN MORLEY • JOHN MORTIMER

SIR CLAUS MOSER • FRANK MUIR • RICCARDO MUTI • PETER NICHOLS • LORD NORWICH • LORD OLIVIER • JOAN PLOWRIGHT • TONY PALMER • ALAN PARKER • SIR PETER PEARS • RONALD PICKUP • HAROLD PINTER • ERIC PORTER • DILYS POWELL • ROBERT POWELL • JONATHAN PRYCE • FREDERIC RAPHAEL • IAN RICHARDSON • TONY RICHARDSON • BRIAN RIX • NICOLA WORG • KEN RUSSELL • WILLY RUSSELL

PRUNELLA SCALES • RONNIE SCOTT • SIR HARRY SECOMBE • MARTIN SHAW • NED SHERRIN • GERRY SOLTI • SIR GEORG SOLTI • JOHNNY SPEIGHT • NORMAN ST JOHN-STEVAS • JANET SUZMAN • BOB SWASH • SIR MICHAEL TIPPETT • SIR JOHN TOOLEY • FELIKS TOPOLSKI • DONALD TRELFORD • IAN WALLACE • DAVID WARNER • GERRY WEISS • TIMOTHY WEST • JOHN WILLIAMS • MALCOLM WILLIAMSON • MICHAEL WINNER • EDWARD WOODWARD • MICHAEL YORK • SUSANNAH YORK

Published by the Greater London Council.

In defence of the arts 131 notables signed this statement which appeared in The Times *in March 1984.*

Richard Course of the League Against Cruel Sports works through the Labour Party and the courts.

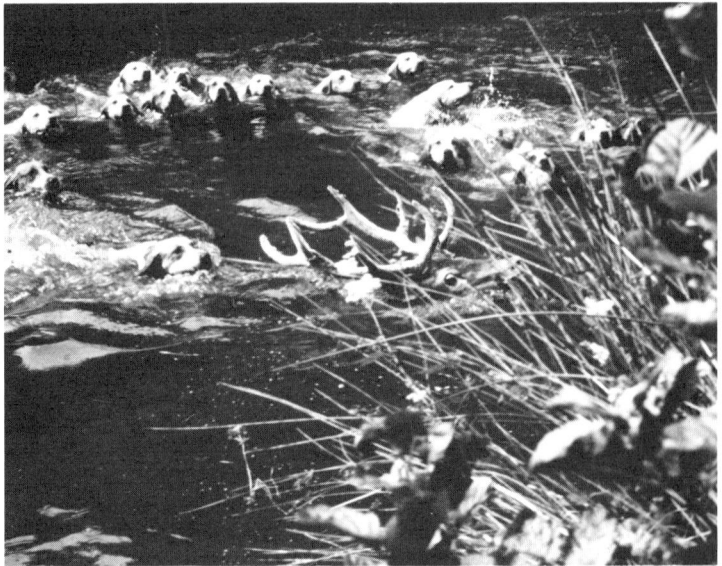

The Devon and Somerset Stag Hounds in action. Their owners have been taken to court by the League Against Cruel Sports.

Robin Grove-White, Director of the Council for the Protection of Rural England. The CPRE is trying to change its conservative, shire-gentry image.

Bryan Forbes, film-maker, actor, author, President of the National Youth Theatre and lobbyist with access to high places.

Hilary Jackson of the Abortion Law Reform Association. Since the Abortion Act was passed in 1967 ALRA has worked tirelessly with other organisations to defend the Act's existence.

Frank Field (left), Director of the Child Poverty Action Group from 1969 until 1979 when he became an MP, seen here with the author outside Parliament. Is the life of an MP more relaxed than that of a lobbyist?

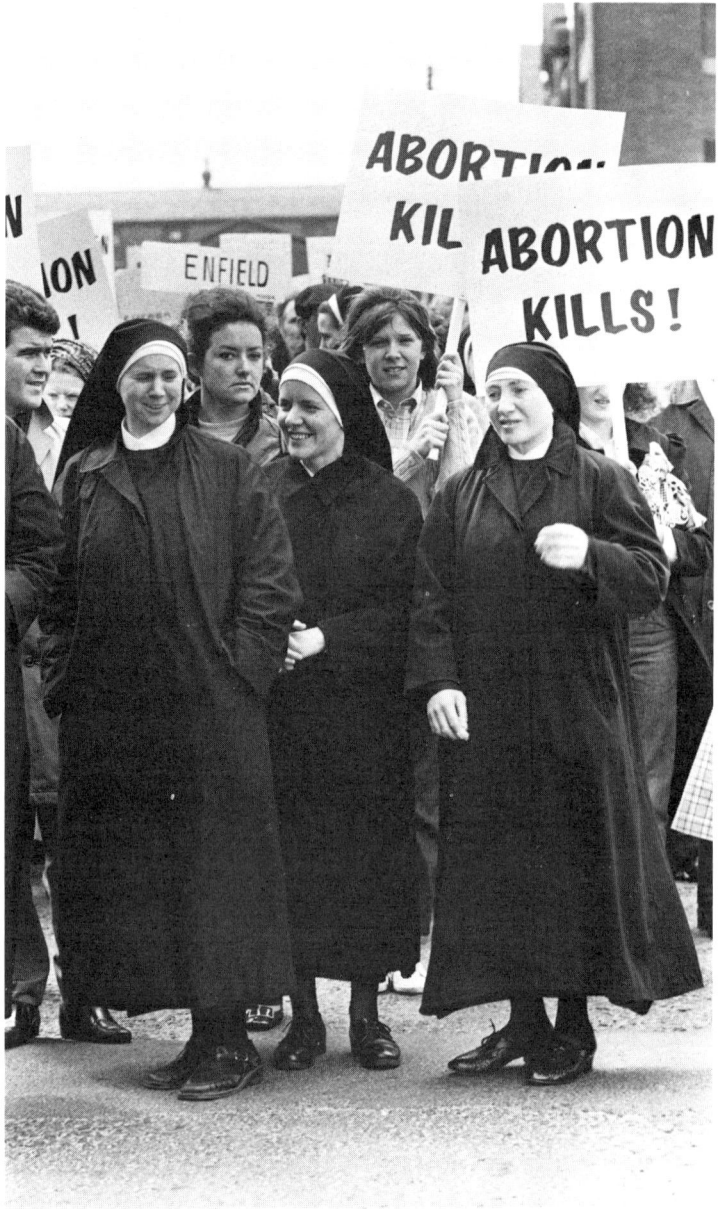

With the abortion lobby one seems to be faced, in the words of Julian Critchley MP, *either by* 'Guardian *women saying their wombs are their own, or nuns concerned with the sanctity of life'.*

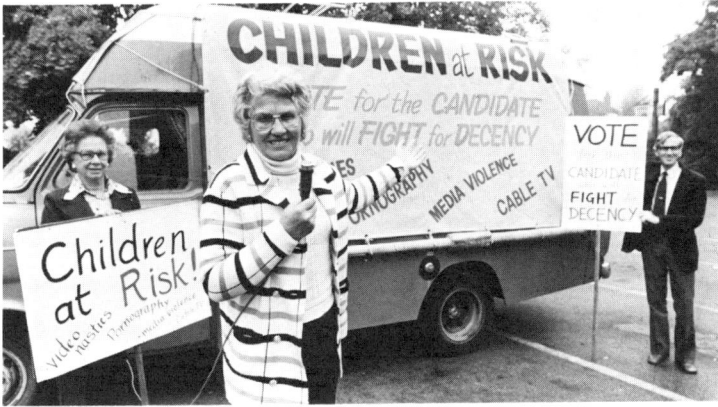

(Above) Mary Whitehouse toured marginal constituencies during the 1983 General Election urging voters to pick the candidate who would fight for decency.

(Left) The price prominent lobbyists pay. When Mary Whitehouse brought a blasphemy action against Gay News in 1977 she became the focus of much abuse. 'It was unbelievable' she says, 'to see the gays marching through London with posters showing the heads of Hitler and me. It was me and Hitler walking through the streets of London.'

Nicholas Fairbairn QC MP and ex-Solicitor-General of Scotland has defended artists such as Anna Kessler, charged with indecency after she had been wheeled naked across the stage as part of a poetry exhibition.

David Tench of the Consumers' Association worked closely with Austin Mitchell MP on the House Buyers Bill, which broke the solicitors' monopoly on conveyancing.

Sir Christopher Hewetson, President of the Law Society 1983/4. The Law Society hired the parliamentary consultancy firm of Charles Barker Watney and Powell Ltd to resist the House Buyers Bill.

Evie Soames, a professional lobbyist and joint Managing Director of Charles Barker Watney and Powell Ltd.

Mike Daube also takes a professional approach to lobbying. He moved from Shelter to become the Director of ASH in 1974 and subsequently advised on the launch of AAA (Action on Alcohol Abuse).

It takes up to 40 dumb animals to make a fur coat.

But only one to wear it.

GREENPEACE

If you don't want animals to be gassed, electrocuted, trapped or strangled, don't buy a fur coat. 16 Graham Street London N1 8LL Tel 01-251 3020

Three forms of pressure: (above) posters persuade; (right) marches get mileage in the media; (below) explosives kill. Secretary of State for Trade and Industry, Norman Tebbit, was a survivor of the bomb which killed five people in the Grand Hotel, Brighton, during the Conservative Party's 1984 Annual Conference. In a week when the bishops of the Church of England had been scolded for bringing religion and morality into politics, the bomb was a forceful reminder of what can happen when morality is left out and political ends are pursued regardless of means.

CARDIFF CND
HISTORIANS FOR THE RIGHT TO WORK
A CONTINUING
JOBS NOT BOMBS
MILTON KEYNES PEACE CAMPAIGN
FALL OUT
CND
STUDENTS UNION
THE NUCLEAR RACE MEANS

4 Pressure outside Parliament

Both Burke and Bryce would have recognised the relevance of lobbying Parliament as described in the preceding chapter. Viscount Bryce (1838–1922), politician and constitutional writer during the late Victorian and early twentieth-century Parliaments, was one of the first writers to see the significance of lobbying in Britain. His definition of the activity, discussed in the Introduction to this book, named Parliament as the exclusive arena for lobbying. Burke also would have approved of lobbying being centred on Parliament; he saw Parliament as the proper forum in which the representatives of the electors could deliberate to make decisions in the national interest.

Burke's eighteenth-century view of the role of Parliament is less valid in late twentieth-century Britain with its mass political parties, and mass electorate. Electors today are less willing to accept elitist assumptions about the role of MPs or the related view which sees electors as deferential and passive. Furthermore, as the corporatists point out, the size and scope of the modern state in a welfare capitalist society has been greatly extended by state intervention in economic policy, industrial control via nationalisation and the development of a welfare role which includes provision of state education, health services and welfare schemes for the ageing, sick, handicapped and unemployed. If we add in changing world dynamics as a variable, then Parliament seems less central to the control of events than do the IMF, NATO and the Common Market. Britain's economy is very dependent on international markets; its defences are intricately linked to the USA so that its ability to act autonomously is seriously reduced from what it was in earlier times when 'Britannia ruled the waves'. A national Parliament in a country which has lost its capacity for independent action is clearly more likely to respond to, rather than determine, world events. Parliament formally ceded some of its sovereignty when Britain signed the Treaty of Rome in 1972. The European Parliament in Strasbourg can now make laws which have priority over British laws as long as Britain is a member of the Common Market. In the words of Tony Benn MP: 'Britain has ceded the power of the purse to the IMF and the EEC, and the power of the sword to the USA'. (*Honourable Members*, BBC TV, 1983)

Pluralists would also reject the version of politics found in the writings of Burke and Bryce. For them power is not something that is fixed and static and located in one or a few of the extant political institutions such as the Crown, the Cabinet or Parliament. For them power is more fluid, less certain and more negotiable with differing actors taking part in the decision-making process on various topics.

One traditional way of examining politics and government derives from the ancient Greek view that government could be divided into three branches: the legislature, the executive and the judiciary. The legislative function was to 'represent' the community and deliberate on matters of public interest and to make laws. The executive function was to carry out the daily organisation and operation of government. The judicial function was carried out by the judges, who acted as arbitrators in disputes and interpreted legal ambiguities or conflicts between laws.

The reification of this tripartite division is such that it is not uncommon in our culture to regard politics as exclusively concerned with matters involving the parliamentary rivalry between political parties, and to see the executive and judicial functions as being aloof from political matters, with civil servants and judges carrying out their tasks in an apolitical fashion. But recognising the virtue in a liberal–democratic state of having judges and government officials who do not act on the basis of personal or systematic political prejudice is not to deny that their activities are political, both in the fundamental sense in that they are involved in public matters, and in a more subtle sense in the way that political assumptions come to shape their routine practices and their interpretations of events and tasks. Hence politics and political lobbying are no longer confined to the parliamentary rivalry between the political parties.

As I have already suggested in the Introduction, it is my view that the British socio-political system is not directed exclusively, or even primarily, from Westminster. To recognise this point is to accept that for lobbying to be effective at national policy level it must simultaneously seek to influence a number of other organisations, or, more accurately, the people who have influence in, or control over, these organisations. Thus the network of the powerful is extended beyond parliamentarians so as to include Prime Ministers, Cabinet members, government ministers, Whitehall bureaucrats, state and public officials, party officials, journalists and news producers. In Chapter 5 I shall consider the relationship between lobby groups and the media. In this chapter I shall be looking at aspects of lobbying which reflect the view that power is not exclusively centred in Parliament by examining four lobbying targets: the executive (both political and administrative), political parties, the courts, and international agencies.

4.1 *Lobbying the executive*

> 'That many extensions of government have proved useful, I acknowledge. But the following points are worth making. Government, including elected Members of Parliament, and members of local authorities, as well as the Civil Service, must now be treated as an interest on their own, as much say, as ICI or the National Union of Mineworkers.' Jo Grimond (*Daily Telegraph*, 13.7.1981)

In Chapter 3 I described two situations where MPS are crucial targets for the activities of lobby groups, firstly, during periods when the government does not have a clear majority, as with the Callaghan Government in the late 1970s, and secondly, on those occasions when a free vote is held on an issue like hanging, abortion or wearing seat belts.

One of the people I interviewed for the TV series *Politics of Pressure* – Sir Charles Cunningham – emphasised the importance of the MP as a target for the lobbyist in a free-vote situation. Sir Charles had been the most senior civil servant – the Permanent Secretary – at the Home Office from 1957 to

1966 during which time capital punishment legislation was first modified and then abolished by a free vote on each occasion:

> 'Therefore, whichever Member promoted a bill had to be sure of a majority of Members to support it on a free vote. He couldn't rely on the whips. For that reason I think that a great deal of effort made by those who were opposed to the death penalty was directed not so much at the Home Office as to the individual Member of Parliament.'

Much more frequently expressed by those interviewed for the *Politics of Pressure*, however, was the view that MPs are basically lobby fodder for the Government. Des Wilson contrasted the benefit of having an MP's support with the benefit of having that of the Prime Minister, the latter giving a campaign a virtual guarantee of success. The dwindling of the power of Parliament with the corresponding growth in the power of the executive was a commonly expressed and regretted view among interviewees of the balance of influence in British political institutions.

Julian Critchley:

> 'The more astute amongst the lobbies realise it is not so much the Member of Parliament who carries weight, it is the minister and, more particularly, the civil servant.'

Andrew Roth:

> 'There is no doubt that power is in the Cabinet, and that it is in the Prime Minister's hands. But there is also a considerable amount of power in a civil servant's hands.'

The late Richard Crossman, a long-serving Labour MP, Cabinet minister and political writer, used the distinction made by Walter Bagehot (the Victorian political writer and analyst) between 'dignified' and 'efficient' parts of the British Constitution to describe Parliament in the 1950s and 1960s. Crossman saw the House of Commons as increasingly coming to resemble the monarchy as a 'dignified' part of the constitution, appearing to legitimate power by gaining public approval but no longer wielding 'effective' power.

How can we explain this growth in the effective power of both the political executive of Cabinet ministers, and the administrative executive of senior civil servants?

The growth in the power of the political executive can be explained by developments in twentieth-century politics. It is illustrated by the way the Government's Whips' Office can ensure regular support amongst MPs for government legislation and motions in support of the Government. Government business is rarely interrupted in the House of Commons. The underlying causes for this exist in the development of nationwide mass political parties in which widespread electoral support is required if a party is to gain office and in the sanctions and rewards available to the whips through the patronage of the Prime Minister. It is the Prime Minister who, after taking advice, decides who is to become Foreign Secretary, who is to receive a peerage or the MBE, or who, in the words of Julian Critchley, 'is to have the privilege of being chauffeured about in a black Austin Princess'. It is the Prime Minister who decides when to resign and call a general election, thus creating the possibility that MPs might lose their much coveted seats. The threat of calling an election (except for those in safe seats) is sufficient to convince all but the most recalcitrant rebel MP to toe the party line.

But it is the growth of the modern political parties, as they evolved after 1918 when the vote was extended to most adults (except women under 30 years of age), that has had most to do with adding to the power of the Prime Minister. Selling the party image began to become much more important. Throughout the democratic world the marketing of politics became a mass phenomenon. Leaders acquired importance, not because they were weak or strong, wise or foolish, but because the party's fortune depended increasingly on them, and even more so when the mass media became the intermediary between voters and leaders. There had, of course, always been the newspapers, but in the 1930s wireless brought in another form of intervention between the electors and their leaders. Then the 1950s saw the beginning of the rise of television politics. Physical appearance became crucial in addition to the sound of the voice. The USA took the lead in this with the 'selling of the President', but Britain, with help from the likes of Saatchi and Saatchi, was not far behind. Today, members of the Cabinet make regular appearances on TV and their faces become well known, whereas how many electors could name more than a few celebrated backbenchers such as Enoch Powell, Cyril Smith or Julian Critchley?

It is not only ambitious MPs who refuse to step out of line for fear of being overlooked as frontbench material. Even Cabinet ministers find lobby groups useful in that they may hold certain beliefs but dare not utter them for political reasons. Des Wilson:

> 'You'd be surprised how many MPs and sometimes even ministers in the governmental party, welcome the pressure group as a way of having something said that they either can't say for technical or political reasons, or are frightened to say. It is well known amongst pressure groups that many Members of Parliament are frightened of the Prime Minister and particularly the new breed of young ambitious conservative MPs who hope maybe to become ministers; they are not going to step out of line. I can remember Dick Crossman, when he was Secretary of State for Social Services, talking to me about pressure groups and he said, "You keep on with Shelter, Des, you're a tremendous asset to me. When I go into the Cabinet Room and we start arguing about resources and someone talks about cutting back on housing, I say to them, 'Do you want Shelter or the Child Poverty Action Group on our backs?'" So in fact ministers quote pressure groups whenever it suits them to do so.'

There is no doubting that an influential member of the Government has immeasurably more power than the ordinary backbencher. In the late 1950s 'Rab' Butler was an influential member of Harold Macmillan's Conservative Government. He was one of the outstanding Home Secretaries of the century and his mark on penal affairs was made in a number of ways. Sir Charles Cunningham describes the impact he made on penal policy:

> 'The origin of the changes in the Prison Rules is to be found in Mr Butler's white paper, *Penal Practice in a Changing Society*. When he became Home Secretary

he was extremely interested in this aspect of his responsibilities. For example, he took the initiative in setting up the Institute of Criminology and financing research on a scale which had never been attempted before, and he wanted, in this white paper, to set out a broad policy for the penal services in this country. In doing that, I think it was made abundantly clear that he and the Home Office at the time regarded rehabilitation in sentencing to be the predominant element.'

In contrast many ministers have less influence than 'Rab' Butler and they can become the butt for lobbyists who are out to discredit them. Mike Daube described in Chapter 3 how he thought the tobacco lobby was effective in bringing about the removal of Sir George Young as a junior minister at the Department of Health and Social Security. Daube's view is supported in a book called *Smoke Ring: the Politics of Tobacco* (1984), in which the author, Peter Taylor, argues that Sir George Young had plans for tough anti-smoking legislation and so became a target for the activities of the tobacco lobby. He claims that this 'smoke ring' of pressure is effective in many countries, including the usa, and states that there is a 'protective circle of political and economic interest that keeps the power of the tobacco industry intact'. Mike Daube gives the following account of what he believes happened:

'As always in these areas you only knew about three per cent of what actually is going on. We certainly knew there was a lot of lobbying within and outside the House of Commons. The tobacco lobby were exceedingly unhappy; suddenly here's a minister who not only believes that something should be done about smoking as a priority, but knows what he wants and manages to persuade his Cabinet minister, the Secretary of State, that they really should act tough. So the tobacco industry and its supporters in the advertising industry and the media organised a great deal of lobbying. There was pressure publicly and privately. mps were organised to sign petitions and to write letters complaining about what he was up to. There were quiet words dropped in people's ears all over the place and there was public criticism. It even got to the stage where it was reported [in the *Daily Mirror*] that the then Minister of State at the DHSS, Gerard Vaughan, was approached by the well-known 'elected' political figure Dennis Thatcher, who asked whether, because of the threat to sports sponsorship by tobacco companies, Gerry Vaughan and his colleagues at the DHSS couldn't [go easy on the issue]! If you have got to Number Ten you haven't done badly in your lobbying.'

Having access to the Prime Minister is a distinct advantage to lobbyists, whether it be through meetings at 10 Downing Street or at Chequers, the Prime Minister's official country residence in the Chilterns. It was at Chequers that Bryan Forbes, actor, writer and head of a large film company who is an active lobbyist on behalf of the theatre, writers and film-makers, was able to express doubts to Mrs Thatcher about changes in the way films were funded. In 1979 a system of capital allowances had been introduced to help raise money for film-making. In the 1984 Budget the Chancellor announced his intention of phasing out these allowances. Bryan Forbes:

'I was surprised that the Conservative Government had phased them out and made my views known as far as the Prime Minister. I took advantage of being invited to lunch at Chequers and button-holed her there. I don't think one should ever abuse hospitality, but the conversation came up . . . the PM asked me what I felt about it, and I said that I felt it was a sad move and I didn't quite understand why it had been made. She listened very politely.'

One attempt to counter-balance the shift of power away from Parliament to the executive was the introduction of a new select committee system in 1979. Parliament had from Victorian times used select committees to investigate major issues and the Public Accounts Committee was one of the most long-standing and effective of these. The 1979 reform resulted in 14 committees being established to monitor the activities of the major government departments. They are able to cross-examine ministers and civil servants responsible for policy in their respective departments, although clashes have occurred as to the degree of information they are entitled to ask for. Some commentators see this development as a crucial opportunity for Parliament to revive its powers by adopting more of a Washington-style approach in which the activities of the executive can be exposed by ruthless, detailed policy cross-examination. Critics of the system suggest, however, that these committees divert attention from the main chamber of the House of Commons. Others suggest they are merely a way of letting off steam with no corresponding effect on policy. Sir Charles Cunningham believes they ought to serve a useful function, but:

> 'I think that, if you were to analyse the results that had flowed from the reports that had been submitted, they wouldn't be able to point to a great deal of action taken on the reports. But I think they perform a valuable function in bringing matters to notice and in keeping departments on their toes.'

Other devices exist through which the executive can be made more open to public and parliamentary scrutiny. One is the establishment of a Royal Commission or Committee of Inquiry to investigate some aspect of the style or content of government operation. But there are those who see it as procrastination or, in David Tench's words, a means of 'burying an issue':

> 'It's a typical way for the Government to bury an issue. It gets them off the hook and they don't have to make any positive response in terms of policy. They appoint a Royal Commission and then take a long time and a lot of money to reach pretty vague and unsatisfactory conclusions.'

Not only does a Royal Commission defuse an issue; it also takes so long to report that, by the time its recommendations are made, public interest may have dwindled and eventually nothing happens at all. Labour MP, Geoffrey Robinson, points to the lack of action after a number of reports by Royal Commissions:

> 'Nothing happened over the Donovan Report or the Finneston Report ... no action was taken by the Government. I was rather dismayed the other day to see a letter in *The Times* calling for a Royal Commission

on the question of education and training and our need to provide more engineers and scientists for industry, which I happen to believe is extremely important. If you confine so important an issue ... to a Royal Commission, it'll just disappear for two or three years.'

Michael Schofield was a member of the Wootton Committee which inquired into the the problem of smoking cannabis and reported in 1969. He comments not only on the inertia that followed the report, but also on the way in which officials from the Home Office dominated some of the discussions:

'In some of the sub-committees the Home Office dominated very much. I remember one committee where people who weren't on the committee spoke more than people who were. Not so with Lady Wootton; she held things very much in control.

It is interesting that in the early days the general atmosphere was, "This will only take six months, we'll just devise some way to deal with this filthy habit!" But by the end attitudes had changed, even amongst those who were anti-cannabis, in view of the sheer weight of the evidence. This says something for this method of government committee. Would that somebody would take some notice of it after it had been reported.'

Obviously lobby groups are keen to get their representatives on any government Committee of Inquiry or Royal Commission. The members are usually selected through recommendations made by government officials to the relevant minister, and representatives of relevant professional interest groups are prime candidates. Anything to do with penal policy, for example, will inevitably have representatives from the judiciary, the magistracy, the police, magistrate's clerks, the prison department and the legal teaching profession. In the unlikely event of there being a lack of suitable suggestions, there is a central register of 'the good and worthy' which can be drawn upon. Sir Charles Cunningham here explains the selection process:

'I think one has a general knowledge of people who are active and respected in the areas of interest that the Committee or Commissions are likely to be concerned with. Ministers at the time may have their own ideas about members that they would regard as suitable. One can also always go to the central register of people known to be available for public duty in a particular area and see whether any names are there that appear to be those of suitable people.'

The Royal Commission on the Provision of Legal Service (the Benson Report) was set up in the mid-1970s and reported in 1979. David Tench remembers the Law Society's hostility until the recommendations were made public:

'When the Royal Commission was set up the Law Society, typical of it, was vociferously opposed to it, particularly its composition, and I can remember reading in the legal press letters from solicitors expressing outrage at how this Royal Commission was packed with people who were hostile to the legal profession and how the outcome of the report could already be regarded as totally unacceptable to the legal profession. Of course in the event it wasn't that way at all.'

The cautious nature of the Benson Report's recommendations and the disappointing non-emergence of radical reforms is explained here by Ole Hansen, Director of Legal Action Group. It was a result, he argues, of the close contact that had been maintained between the Commission and the Law Society:

'It's been well documented that before the Commission made any recommendation it would go round the corner to the Law Society in Chancery Lane, for instance on education and training, and say: "This is what we've got in mind, how do you react?" Therefore, there were a series of compromises between people on the Royal Commission and the Law Society.'

Hansen sees the establishment of a Royal Commission as a ploy by the administration to avoid public pressure for change:

'It's very easy to be led up a blind alley as I think we were by the Royal Commission. The typical Royal Commission ploy is that pressure builds up for change, so they set up the Royal Commission which stops discussion for about three or four years. You can't do anything while it is sitting. By the time the report appears they hope everyone has forgotten about it and it'll go away and of course that is exactly what happened.'

Sitting on Royal Commissions will be a senior civil servant who will act as the Commission's secretary and will ensure that the 'right people' will be approached to submit evidence and also that the departmental views of the relevant ministries are taken into account.

Officially, it is the job of the Permanent Secretary of a department to make sure that the Commission and its political master – the minister – know the relevant arguments and facts. Sir Charles Cunningham explains:

'It is the duty, I think, of a department, and certainly of its Permanent Secretary, to present a problem to a minister in an objective and analytical way and to put both sides of the case. It is true that you can't fail to indicate what your own view is, but you would feel you were letting yourself down if you didn't present the alternative approach to the problem and the alternative solution of it in as fair and objective a way as you can.'

But given the size and complexity of the modern government department it would be most unusual if the minister were able to keep up with all the issues concerning his or her department. The Home Office, for example, has responsibilities ranging from the police, prisons and immigration to broadcasting and control of firearms. During the period from 1900 to 1984 there have been 33 different political heads, i.e. Home Secretaries, but only 12 Permanent Secretaries. This longevity amongst official civil servants who head the department gives them a technical expertise that ensures that the department's view will probably prevail on all but those issues in which there is a clear political will shown by the minister and the Government of the day. During Sir Charles Cunningham's nine years at the Home Office he worked with four Home Secretaries: 'Rab' Butler (1957–62), Henry Brooke (1962–64), Frank Soskice (1964–65) and Roy Jenkins (1965–67).

Sir Charles recognises a similar problem experienced by the ordinary backbench MP in trying to keep in touch with administrative matters:

'I think it must be very difficult for the individual Member of Parliament to keep in close and continuous touch with all that is going wrong in a major department and if he has to try to do this for a number of departments, it must be very difficult indeed.'

The sheer size of the public sector makes scrutiny difficult. In the 1980s there are over half a million civil servants, to which can be added five and a half million public sector employees in the armed forces, police, schools, local authorities, the NHS, the nationalised industries and public corporations. On the question of the balance of power between the Home Secretary and the department's Permanent Secretary Sir Charles declared:

'I never thought of the relationship as one of power on one side and lack of power on the other, but as a joint effort on the part of the Home Secretary and his department to come to the best conclusion they could come to and on any matter they had to consider.'

Regardless of the question of the balance of power between the political and administrative heads of a government department, it is obvious that the administrator is a useful person to have on your side if you are a lobby group. One occasion when a department comes into contact with lobby groups is when it is helping to construct a private Member's bill. As many of the details of policy are very technical drafting legislation has its own legal complications and the department often offers its expertise. Dr Geoffrey Alderman:

'A great deal of legislation is thrashed out in Whitehall. Much of it is technical. Parliament simply hasn't the expertise with these matters. That's not to say that Parliament doesn't have a voice, and, if it so wishes, a veto. But we ought not to think any longer of the House of Commons and the House of Lords as primarily legislating chambers. That's not their role. Their role is to put their stamp of approval, which may be wholehearted or may be qualified, upon legislation which has been hammered out elsewhere.'

The Home Office can play an important role in providing drafting assistance to private Members who wish to promote 'acceptable legislation' in areas for which the Home Office is responsible. Sir Charles Cunningham:

'We did this, for example, with the Death Penalty Bill, with the bill on homosexuality, with the Abortion Bill. These were all private Members' measures where the Home Office in each case worked very closely with the promoter.'

Some lobby groups have an established working relationship with a government department. Others are regarded as outsiders. Mick Ryan in his book, *The Acceptable Pressure Group* (1978) makes the distinction between those groups recognised as 'acceptable' by a government department – for example, the Howard League's insider status at the Home Office – and the outsider status of more radical pressure groups such as RAP (Radical Alternatives to Prison).

Sir Charles Cunningham, referring to the Howard League in particular, reflects on the advantage for a department of working with lobby groups with 'insider status':

'One has got to try and judge how policies and legislation are working out. A pressure group can provide some indication of areas in which there is at least a degree of interest. The department then has to try and assess how representative the pressure group is or how good its arguments for change are, or what degree of support it is likely to have among members of the public and Members of Parliament. This all feeds information and knowledge of reaction into the complex of information the department uses in judging the effectiveness of its policy or of its legislation. The pressure group can also, just by being there, stimulate a degree of debate about a topic – which I think is healthy.

The Howard League, of course, is a body of long standing and it has a very high reputation. The Home Office always had the most cordial relations with the Howard League. At the time we are talking about [1957–66] our objectives were in a sense the same because this was a period when the department was trying to emphasise the main object of penal treatment was rehabilitation rather than retribution. It was a time when both the Howard League and the Home Office were anxious to reduce the number of people who went to prison, particularly for short periods, and

I think it was the Howard League that at one point took the initiative in suggesting a committee of enquiry into short sentences of imprisonment, which led the Home Office to refer their problem to the Advisory Council on the Treatment of Offenders. We had close contact with Hugh Klare as the Secretary of the Howard League and of course the Home Secretary was constantly seeing Sir George Benson, who was for many years the Chairman.'

One group that did not have insider status at the Home Office until recently was Mary Whitehouse's National Viewers' and Listeners' Association. Mary Whitehouse:

'We found the permanent staff at the Home Office over the years were almost totally unwilling to listen or to take into account what we were saying. I have to say, in all fairness, that over the last two to three years, particularly since Mrs Thatcher has shown herself to be so concerned and to be so determined to get some action in this field, the Civil Service have decided they'd better sit up and listen a little bit and be a bit more flexible.'

Whatever form of contact a lobby group attempts to set up with the Civil Service, it has to be done carefully. In this country civil servants claim, with some justification, to be independent and incorruptible, and permanent officials will not take kindly to the slightest hint of bribery, threat or demand. Sir Charles Cunningham states that, even during the height of the anti-hanging campaign, 'I don't think we were under any great pressure.'

Andrew Roth refers to the Civil Service's reputation for incorruptibility and discusses the possible implications for lobbyists of the trend for more senior civil servants to accept posts as consultants or managers in business soon after their resignation from government work:

'The Civil Service is very jealous for the most part about its reputation. But they are not 100 per cent incorruptible because if you are a civil servant in the defence department, someone in the defence industry might say: "You have a tremendous expertise so when you retire we would love to give you a job working for us. That would help us to work for the Government more effectively". That can happen. That's a more subtle form of corruption ... If you are expecting to work for a particular company, I suppose there is a sub-conscious desire to make yourself look better and perhaps nudge contracts in their direction.'

From 1979 to 1983 the Ministry of Defence received 999 applications from senior military and civil personnel seeking to resign to take up business posts, the great bulk of which were with 'departmentally related industries'. This development has in recent years led the House of Commons Select Committee on the Treasury and Civil Service to set up an inquiry under the chairmanship of Austin Mitchell. Its report, published in 1984, *Acceptance of Outside Appointments by Crown Servants*, stated: 'The tradition, independence and impartiality of the Civil Service is in danger of being eroded or compromised in the eyes of the public'. The report points out the potential for impropriety when a civil servant moves to an appointment with a firm with whom he or his department had dealings. It quotes from the House of Commons Select Committee on Expenditure's 11th Report (1976–77): 'There has been public criticism implying that the prospect of ...... outside jobs can be dangled before civil servants as an influence upon them before they leave the service'. The report recommends that civil servants should not on retirement or resignation take up a post closely connected with a department's work until five years has elapsed.

4.2 *Persuading the parties*

Interest groups have frequently provided the historical basis for the emergence and evolution of political parties in western industrial society. Trade union interests established the Labour Party in 1900 whilst the Conservative Party over a longer period was the representative of property and business. Some lobby groups are thus inextricably and traditionally linked to a political party. The question for others is, should they align themselves with a party? And, if so, how can they influence party policy?

There are two answers to this question. On the side of the non-partisan approach is Charles Secrett of Friends of the Earth (FOE) and Mike Daube, previously with ASH. Charles Secrett says of FOE's strategy:

'We can approach government backbenchers in a way that, for instance, the official Opposition never can, because we are a non-party political organisation. We let our facts speak for ourselves rather than any party allegiance.'

Mike Daube:

'If you're working on a public health campaign, then you can't afford to be politically aligned. We had an all-party group in the House of Commons with something over 100 Members of Parliament towards the end and I don't think any of them knew which way I voted in elections. I think it's absolutely crucial for somebody in my position to be non-partisan.'

Larry Gostin of the NCCL takes the same view as Mike Daube, and firmly believes that identification with one political party is a mistake, despite the fact that most of the NCCL members are concerned with liberal and radical aspects of civil rights. He says: 'It means the only time you will influence policy is when your particular political party is in power.' Larry Gostin's commitment to an 'all-party' approach was to prove successful when MPs from across the political spectrum supported MIND when the Mental Health Bill went through Parliament in 1983.

The opposite point of view about the cross-party approach is argued by Richard Course, the Director of the League Against Cruel Sports (LACS). In the 1984 spring edition of LACS journal *Cruel Sports* he wrote an article entitled 'Why You Should Join a Political Party'. In it he encouraged the members of LACS to join political parties and promote the objectives of LACS from the inside. He is attempting to convert the middle-class animal welfare campaigners into a more effective political group by moving the organisation into a partisan commitment to the Labour Party:

'I think it's absolutely right that all pressure groups should take their policies and programmes to the various political parties and we took ours to all three of the major parties. The Labour Party adopted it; obviously we used whatever friends we had. We tried the same thing in the Liberal Party and to be fair the Liberal Party did agree with us and took it up as an issue. But the control of the Liberal manifesto is not in the hands of the party conference.'

The Labour Party conference agreed to include the following resolution in their 1979 and 1983 general election manifestos: 'Hare coursing, fox hunting and all forms of hunting with dogs will be made illegal', a commitment which caused LACS to make an election donation of £50,000 to the Labour Party. (This led to a court case and the money was returned.) This means that LACS will support the return of a Labour Government with its manifesto promise to introduce anti-hunting legislation, even though this might mean working in elections against Conservative MPs who are renowned anti-hunters. During the making of the TV series *Politics of Pressure* we received a letter from Richard Course which set out LACS' new political determination to ally its fortunes with the return of a Labour Government even if it means campaigning for Labour MPs who hunt, however few. He wrote:

'Clearly the political aspects of our work are the most important, particularly bearing in mind that we need a manifesto commitment to succeed. In order to win, we must for example, try to unseat Janet Fookes, Tory MP, who is perhaps one of the best animal campaigners in the House, and at the same time hope that John Ryman MP, retains his seat, although he is the only Labour MP who hunts and regularly rides with the exclusive Quorn Hunt.'

The Labour Party's constitution delegates the formation of the election manifesto to the annual party conference. So if a manifesto commitment is sought, any lobby group must be prepared to take on the arduous and long-winded process of getting resolutions accepted by constituency Labour Parties or affiliated trade unions. Then comes the protracted process of deciding composite motions for the conference to debate which reflect broadly the level of total resolutions submitted. Furthermore, attracting the support of trade unions with large block votes can be a time-consuming business;

this requires lobbying union branches throughout the country and at the union annual conferences before the Labour Party conference.

Richard Course and LACS supporters worked hard to get the anti-hunting proposal into the Labour manifesto. This involved working deftly within the Labour Party:

> 'We took it from branch level right through to constituency level and then on to conference. We took the motion down to conference with an exhibition and lobbying material. We spoke to the MPs and ordinary delegates.'

Although time-consuming and frustrating to achieve, the manifesto commitment could be crucial should the Labour Party get back into office. Frank Field reinforces the point:

> 'Anybody who listened to Dick Crossman decades and decades ago would know he always told lobbyists in their early days that the crucial thing is to get your commitment into the manifesto, because that is the map and compass with which ministers are guided, with which they can fight their departments, with which they will be fighting their Cabinet for money and parliamentary time to see part of that programme through.'

Conference votes and resolutions are not the means of establishing the manifesto programme in the Conservative Party. Even so lobbyists can work to ensure manifesto commitments. The 1983 Conservative manifesto promised measures to control video nasties. This promise is being fulfilled by the Government's support for Graham Bright's private Member's bill. The National Viewers' and Listeners' Association have campaigned with much success within the Conservative Party. In 1983 Mary Whitehouse went to Blackpool to lobby delegates at the annual Conservative Party conference. NVALA had compiled an eight-minute tape from what they considered to be four of the worst video nasties. This was shown in a hall outside the main conference. Mary Whitehouse was surprised at the high attendance at the screenings: '... those who came were absolutely shaken to the core, and then, given that, we wrote to the Party leaders.'

With the party conference playing a different role in the policy-formulating process in each of the parties the reasons for lobbyists going to the different conferences will vary. Although the Labour Party conference is nominally the most formally influential, if the Labour Party is not in office then this can result in a good deal of wasted effort. Most lobbyists will want to go to the conference of the party in power. Andrew Roth, who has been attending the party conferences regularly since 1950, explains the advantage of the conference for the lobbyist:

> 'There are PR men for various national organisations who spend their time button-holing ministers [because] a conference is much more relaxed and open than the House of Commons is, and when a minister is here, he is away from his desk, he is away from the surrounding wall of civil servants and people who make up his diary, therefore he is more accessible for a drink or persuasion'.

During the more relaxed atmosphere of the annual party conference, ministers can be found mingling informally with delegates and lobbyists. In the hope of discussing their Right-to-Work Campaign, eight workers from Cammell Laird Shipyard travelled down from Birkenhead to Brighton for the 1984 Tory Party conference. They found the minister responsible for the shipbuilding industry, Norman Lamont, Minister of State in the Department of Trade and Industry, in the Grand Hotel and put their arguments to him.

Of course the approach might vary according to party ideology. Larry Gostin believes that it helps if an organisation like the NCCL is known to the party activists who attend conference. In 1984 the NCCL attended all four of the major party conferences. They organised fringe meetings, had a book stall and sought to meet MPs and party workers. They were also careful to emphasise aspects of their campaigning which they considered to be most compatible with a particular party's ideology. On the subject of civil liberties this can take some thinking out, as Larry Gostin explains:

> 'At the Liberal Party conference we are emphasising anti-discrimination. At the Conservative Party conference we are emphasising privacy and criminal justice, and at the Labour Party conference we are

emphasising trade union rights. The whole concept of civil liberties to my great regret is bitterly divided along party lines and if you talk to any particular political party, they think that they hold the monopoly of civil liberties in one particular area.

In certain parties it is the right to work, or the right not to have to join a trade union if it is a closed shop. If you talk to other parties, it is the right to join a trade union.'

Another supporter of the all-party approach to lobbying is Ken Livingstone. He toured all four of the party conferences in 1983 and 1984, as well as the TUC and CBI annual conferences. Although a staunch Labour Party member he was prepared to seek support on an all-party basis to help with the 'Save the GLC' campaign. He explains why he bothered to lobby the SDP conference, a party which returned only six MPs after the 1983 general election:

'Although there are only six MPs, there are something like about 30 or 40 peers and our key to success in amending the Government's abolition of elections bill was actually getting all the peers out and we needed every one. You can't write off any section of support when you are trying to keep an organisation like the GLC.

4.3 *Campaigning through the courts*

Mary Whitehouse and NVALA were not only successful in their lobbying efforts at the 1983 Conservative Party conference; they have also used the courts to promote their cause. One occasion led to the 'blasphemy' trial against *Gay News* in 1977. Then in October 1980 Michael Bogdanov's version of *The Romans in Briton* opened at the National Theatre, with a scene showing a Roman soldier attempting sodomy. Mary Whitehouse this time brought a prosecution on the grounds of obscenity. The trial at the Old Bailey in 1982 lasted only three days before the prosecution was dropped. More recently Mary Whitehouse was involved in going to court because of the public broadcasting of the film

Scum. In June 1983 Channel 4 broadcast *Scum*, a film about borstals which included some violent scenes. The NVALA's claim was that the Independent Broadcasting Authority had breached their duties as defined in the 1981 Broadcasting Act in allowing an 'offensive' film to be shown on television. *Scum* had previously been banned by the BBC.

Although the legal case was concerned with one film, NVALA was actually attempting to influence the IBA over the broader question of broadcasting policy. NVALA's counsel in the High Court was Mr John Smith QC, who submitted that:

> 'Important principles underly this motion. It is Mrs Whitehouse's contention, and that of her Association, that over a long period of time the IBA have failed, sometimes flagrantly, in their statutory duty to protect the public in respect of late-night independent television.'

The High Court action which started on 1 February 1984 resulted in some legal action in that the Court considered that the Director-General of Channel 4 had erred. He had failed to refer the film to the IBA for a decision on whether to broadcast it. But the Court did not accept the argument that showing *Scum* was unlawful. Since the IBA intends to appeal, the issue of 'offensive' television will continue to be raised on the back of the legal hearings associated with this case.

The main disadvantage for a lobby group like NVALA of using the courts is cost. High Court hearings and subsequent appeals can be very costly as they are prolonged over many years and incur the expense of highly paid barristers. The advantages are that they can have an instrumental and immediate impact, if successful, in changing the policy or operations of, for instance, a public authority like the IBA. But even if the process is not successful in a legal sense, it might still prove worthwhile because of the associated publicity. If the issue of a legal action is skilfully chosen, if it has the quality of being 'newsworthy', then a lobby group can generate a lot of public and official attention for its cause. The subsequent series of appeals can mean a regular West-End revival and a re-run of the issues which will probably attract an audience bigger than Noel Coward's *Hayfever* ever did.

One recent case which shows how a legal dispute can help set a lobby in motion and sustain its progress is that involving Victoria Gillick. A Roman Catholic mother of 10, she objected to the possibility that her daughters might be prescribed a contraceptive pill under the age of 16 without her prior knowledge and consent. In January 1981 she wrote to her Area Health Authority seeking an assurance that this would not happen. They refused to give a categorical assurance on the grounds that consultation between doctor and patient, even those under 16 years of age, is confidential. The Area Health Authority pointed out that it was operating in accord with DHSS policy guidelines.

Mrs Gillick decided to challenge DHSS policy. She argued that because it is illegal for a girl under 16 to have sexual intercourse then the medical provision of contraceptives was encouraging illegal behaviour, which is proscribed by Section 28 of the Sexual Offences Act 1956.

In July 1983 the case was heard in the High Court. Mrs Gillick lost. The judge ruled that children under 16 were entitled to receive contraceptive advice without their parents' knowledge. Mrs Gillick then decided to appeal against the decision in a higher court.

The battle was gaining momentum. There was full media coverage of the case and background stories which invariably included a photograph captioned 'Roman Catholic Mother Of 10 With Some Of Her Children!' The battle-lines were being drawn. On the one side was the DHSS, the British Medical Association and the Family Planning Association – all respected and established powerful lobby groups. On the other side emerged a new alliance of MPs and representatives of the 'moral right wing' opposed to what they saw as a further decline in sexual standards for young children and a threat to the absolute right of parents to decide what is best for their offspring. By November 1983 they had been rallied to fight back against the DHSS policy.

By the beginning of November 200 MPs had signed a motion, and 300,000 people a petition, asking for parents to have a legal right to be consulted before their daughters under the age of 16 were prescribed contraceptives. On 9 November the Health Minister, Kenneth Clarke, in a written answer to a parliamentary question, replied that he would not review departmental policy until the appeal against the earlier court decision had been heard.

On 11 November, Mrs Gillick achieved celebrity status in the world of British lobby politics. She appeared on TV-AM television and the Jimmy Young Show and then met Dr Gerard Vaughan at the House of Commons. (He had been Minister of Health when the policy was first formulated.) Unfortunately, celebrity status in politics means that unpleasant facts about your past will be used against you by your opponents. In February 1984 *Searchlight*, an anti-racist magazine, revealed Mrs Gillick's earlier involvement in a right-wing, anti-immigration group called Powellright. She and her husband had written a letter on the subject of Ugandian Asians in which they expressed their disapproval of the Government admitting 'yet more coloured aliens for settlement into Great Britain'. Mrs Gillick claimed that this letter had been written a long time previously and that she had now changed her mind on repatriation, but some damage to her public image was done. Another set-back for the campaigners was that the Roman Catholic hierarchy would not lend its support. In April 1984 Cardinal Hume announced that he would not support Mrs Gillick's court action, but wrote to her saying:

> 'The particular issue which you have brought before the courts has, however, as many have recognised, wider implications for the role of law, medical practice and social welfare in a pluralistic society.'

Once the mud-slinging had started, Mrs Gillick slung her own by calling on the Charity Commissioners to revoke the charitable status of the Family Planning Association. She claimed that the association was acting as a political pressure group by lobbying against her campaign to change DHSS policy.

The argument will continue and the system of court appeals will ensure the issue is kept alive. The appeal hearing was postponed from November 1983 to April, then July 1984 and finally set for November 1984. In the meantime, Sir Bernard Braine's Early Day Motion in the House of Commons received 110 signatures in support of Mrs Gillick's attempt to change government policy and accepted medical practice. Counter-mobilisation led to 125 MPs signing a motion in favour of keeping the policy guidelines of the DHSS as they were.

The League Against Cruel Sports is a lobby group which has had to defend itself in the courts. When it tried to donate £50,000 to the Labour Party's campaign fund during the 1983 General Election, it was taken to court, and the judge ruled that the Memorandum of Association governing the legal status of the League did not permit political donations.

But the League also uses the courts to work *for* their cause, for example to restrict hunting in the countryside. Richard Course, the Director of LACS, explains:

> 'There is damage inflicted by maybe 200 or 300 horses riding across the countryside – damage to crops, damage to fences . . . If people don't want them on their land, they should be able to keep them off. But the law of trespass is a civil not a criminal matter and it takes an awful lot of money and an awful lot of will to take a hunt to court. After one or two court actions, a landow-ner can then apply for an injunction to keep the hunt off his land. That is very expensive and not a lot of land-owners are prepared to go to that extent . . . So we do it for them. Across the country that has resulted in a lot of our countryside being prohibited to hunts. I think the injunctions are the important part, because an act of trespass will only bring in £5, £10 or £15 damages.'

The League is currently seeking an injunction against the biggest stag hunt in the country. The League bought land on Exmoor for a sanctuary and is now trying to stop the Devon and Somerset Stag Hounds crossing its property; it has already obtained an interim injunction and has now set aside £20,000 to cover the cost of legal proceedings which will be heard at Bristol High Court. An expensive operation, but, if it succeeds, one which could be a crucial step towards preventing hunts crossing private property, and prove to be a successful lobby tactic.

In 1984 the NCCL are using the courts to challenge the seizure of 200 books by custom officers from the London bookshop, Gay's the Word. This was part of a series of seizures of allegedly obscene homosexual publications by the police and customs. The NCCL is challenging this action by claiming that it is censorship of a minority group's reading material. If they lose before the magistrates in London they are prepared to pursue the matter to the European Court of Human Rights.

Finally, the use of courts by lobby groups is comparatively underdeveloped in this country compared with that in the USA. Dr Geoffrey Alderman explains one reason why this is the case and provides an insight as to why it might change in the future:

'I think there is a fundamental difference between an American pressure group going to a federal court or even the Supreme Court and a British pressure group going to a court of law in this country. The constitution of the United States cannot be changed very easily. And if a pressure group in the United States wins a legal victory based upon, let us say, the Supreme Court's interpretation of the law, then that is a victory which cannot be easily overturned. If a pressure group wins a victory in a British court of law and that victory is not really to the liking of the Government or a section of the Government or a political party, it's a relatively easy matter to have the law changed. Therefore pressure groups have less confidence in the British legal system than American pressure groups do in the American constitution. But a British pressure group has another alternative. It may go to Strasbourg to the European court, and that is really the nearest thing to a constitution – the European Convention on Human Rights – which a British Government will ignore at its peril. Therefore, winning a victory at Strasbourg will have implications which it may be beyond the power of a British Government or British politicians to reverse by themselves.'

4.4 *International co-operation*

The reform of penal policy is not a new lobby activity. The late eighteenth century was a period when individuals such as John Howard were able to identify penal problems and propose reforms. But penal policy has never been a popular topic amongst the populace, politicians or administrations. It involves few votes and many pitfalls. Reforms were passed regularly after John Howard's time, but very slowly, until, that is, the 1970s, when a number of decisions taken by the European Court of Human Rights quickened the pace of change in the area of prisoners' rights.

Since the Golder case (the first case concerning prisoners' rights to be heard at Strasbourg) in 1975 there has been a steady stream of decisions which have improved prison inmates' rights. Under the pressure of cases submitted to Strasbourg, the legal position of inmates has been overturned from the traditional view that prisoners have no rights unless specified by law, to a view recently expressed in the *Raymond* v. *Honey* case (1981) by Lord Justice Wilberforce 'that if there is nothing in the Prison Act denying the rights of prisoners then they should be permitted'.

It is not just prisoners' rights that have been referred to Strasbourg. Disputes as varied as the mistreatment of prisoners in the H-block in Northern Ireland, and the use of corporal punishment and censorship are well within the liberal civil-liberties tradition on human rights. More unusual is the Duke of Westminster's determination to challenge the statutory rights of tenants to purchase their rented properties from his company by taking the issue to Strasbourg.

The Court of Human Rights is just one of a gradually extending range of European institutions that are increasingly affecting British national policy decisions. Britain signed the European Convention on Human Rights in 1950, well before joining the Common Market. Signing the Treaty of Rome in 1972 then allowed institutions other than the Court of Human Rights to intervene in what were previously purely internal matters in British politics.

The organisation of the European Community centres on two institutions: the European Parliament at Strasbourg and the European Commission in Brussels and Luxembourg. The executive tasks carried out by the Commission are spread amongst a number of directorates. This has provided lobbyists with another possible layer of incorporated status. For example, the Director of CPRE, Robin Grove-White, is an active participant in the European Environmental Bureau

(EEB). Through this committee environmental groups have begun to challenge the EEC's Common Agricultural Policy, which they regard as having damaging consequences for the European countryside through its effects on farming practices. This European element in CPRE lobbying means that increasing attention is given to activity in Brussels. Robin Grove-White:

> 'We have a small office in Brussels. There are representative organisations from all the 10 member states such as the Friends of the Earth, CPRE, the Royal Society for the Protection of Birds. I was in Paris recently because there is a French President of the Council of Ministers at the moment. We are negotiating very hard with the French Government to get items on the agenda of the Council of Ministers on agricultural issues. We worked very intensively to influence the Commission in Brussels, especially the Director of Agriculture and the Director of the Environment. I think that over the last 10 years environment policy has actually been one of the success areas of the European Community.'

The European Parliament is the other crucial target. Mary Whitehouse feels that she has convinced the Parliament to adopt a resolution which is tougher than Graham Bright's proposed bill on video nasties in Britain. The Council of Europe held a conference on pornography in the early 1980s and at Assisi in Italy more recently on video nasties. The reports of those conferences both called for legislation on these matters. In May 1984 the European Parliament adopted a resolution on the Marketing of Violence and Horrific Video Cassettes, which called on the Commission to consider legislation to combat the video market in pornography. Mrs Whitehouse is wholly in approval.

Many lobby groups realise today that their lobbying horizon has to extend beyond the boundaries of the UK and the EEC. Their concerns are international because the problems which arouse their interest are not restricted to national territories and require international co-operation to control. In the environmental field the European Environmental Bureau may ban the use of certain pesticides throughout Europe. But if European countries import foodstuff from

Third World countries where there is no ban and on whom the chemical companies can dump their extra supplies of pesticides at a price commercially viable to the Third World, then European food supplies will still be affected by harmful chemicals.

Charles Secrett of FOE elaborates upon the reason why environmental groups adopt an international perspective in their lobbying:

'The thing about environmental philosophy and environmental action is that it doesn't try to demarcate problems, whether it's saving the whales, acid-rain, marine pollution or nuclear power and alternative renewable energy sources. These are international problems; they are not defined by geographical boundaries. We all live on one planet – the point about environment pressure groups is that they try and stress this. They show the destruction of tropical rain forests and then point out that if the forests disappear there is a very good possibility that global climatic patterns will change. So there's this inter-relationship on an international level. This is why we campaign at Friends of the Earth on international issues as well as the single national issues. Friends of the Earth have branches in 26 different countries and this link-up provides for very effective lobbying. Environmental problems are so huge and so ingrained within a system of international relationships, at an economic and political level, that they cannot possibly be solved on a purely domestic front. People say the United Nations is the nearest thing we have to international government and it doesn't work, but I think in the future people are going to see that the way human-kind can benefit most is by nations acting in co-operation. That is something that environmental groups are trying above all to foster and to enhance.'

International co-operation is therefore essential for lobby groups concerned with worldwide problems. A further reason for international lobby group co-operation arises when their opponents have an international structure. When at ASH, Mike Daube had to deal with a tobacco industry with world-wide connections, a world-wide system of production and world-wide markets. So he co-operated with American health groups who were attempting to get smoking restriction extended in the USA and on one occasion went to Washington to appear as an expert witness at a senate hearing on health warnings. The tobacco industry had brought in an 'international expert' and so the American pressure group needed an expert of their own at short notice. Says Daube: 'I was immensely impressed by the sheer professionalism of the tobacco lobby.' Combatting that professionalism required equal effort and co-operation from the health lobby groups if they were to be successful. This kind of co-operation can be aided by international conferences and bilateral meetings which promote mutual understanding.

Mutual education is one advantage of international co-operation. Another is that events in a foreign country can provide an early warning of what might happen domestically in the future. For this reason Mary Whitehouse keeps in contact with American lobby groups concerned with video pornography.

> 'We have international links and, particularly, a lot of links with the United States, so that we get fed information about what is happening before it actually breaks here. This was very true of the video nasties. We knew about them and were able to study them and know what their names were, because they appeared in the States before they ever came here.'

In conclusion, the international dimensions of modern politics have three implications for lobby groups. Firstly, international agencies like the EEC and the UN provide lobby groups with a new forum in which to raise issues and exert pressure on both the international community and the national governments who belong to those agencies. Secondly, international co-operation can provide a stimulus, support and, most importantly, an additional source of information to give lobbyists an advantage they normally lack when dealing with government. Thirdly, the international nature of many of the world's problems means that a solution can only be found through international efforts, and lobby groups might provide a lead when governments are slow to act.

5 *Artful lobbying*

In March 1984 the Arts Council published its annual report which in this year was entitled *The Glory of the Garden*. In the period up to its publication there had been much media speculation about the effects of spring-cleaning in the world of publicly funded arts. The lobbying and controversies surrounding that report will be examined in this chapter, as will the way in which the world of politics and the arts interact with each other with reference to the topics of funding and censorship. As these topics tend to generate a good deal of media interest I felt this to be an appropriate section of the book to discuss the role of the media in general: to look at the functions of the media; the constraints under which it operates; and the significance of 'image' in politics. This concluding chapter also contains a caveat as a reminder that not everyone regards lobbying as a useful political activity – a view which challenges many of the assumptions of those who were interviewed in the course of writing this book.

5.1 *'The Glory of the Garden'*

It is 39 years since the Arts Council was formed and there may have been a time during 1984 when its Chairman, Sir William Rees-Mogg, must have wondered how much longer it would survive. Under threat from a Government wishing to cut public expenditure and with more than its usual share of internal wrangling, the Arts Council published its policy document *The Glory of the Garden* – the name of a Kipling poem – on 30 March 1984. The acclaimed radical re-think of the Council's role and its re-distribution of funding so as to benefit the arts in the provinces more than in London was in the end less significant than the realisation that the Arts

Council had successfully side-stepped a threat to its existence.

The Arts Council was formed in 1945. It took on the role of CEMA (pronounced the same as the medium-paced ball in cricket) – the Council for the Encouragement of Music and Arts. This was a war-time attempt to stimulate cultural interest amongst the public, its most celebrated success being the series of lunch-time concerts in the National Gallery. It was a Government-subsidised activity and the brain-child of the King's College don and economist, John Maynard Keynes, who became the Arts Council's first Chairman.

This innovation in public-funded arts came at a time when many new areas of community activity were being brought under government control and subsidy. In 1945 this was generally regarded as a benign development that had emerged mainly as a consequence of war-time experience with collectivist experiments such as rationing and planning. This spirit of collectivist endeavour continued after the war and resulted in, and was reinforced by, the unexpected landslide victory of the Labour Party in the 1945 General Election. Social planning and reconstruction penetrated all walks of life. The Government under Clement Attlee embarked on a five-year period that witnessed the nationalisation of large sectors of British industry – coal, railways, iron and steel – and the establishment of public bodies, such as the National Health Service.

The arts were also affected by this new enthusiasm for public intervention. However, to avoid the problem of direct political manipulation the Arts Council was formed, which, like the BBC and the University Grants Committee, was accountable to, but not directly controlled by, government. Bryan Appleyard, *The Times* art correspondent and author of *The Culture Club* (1984) comments: 'The Arts Council essentially was a way of laundering government money'.

In like vein, the National Film Finance Corporation was founded in 1949 to administer public subsidies for the film industry.

The incorporation of artistic activities into the 1951 Festival of Britain was, says Bryan Appleyard, a reflection of the new status that the arts had been accorded. Since the war, he writes: 'The arts were on the national agenda, though only shakily pencilled in.'

The Arts Council grew steadily in scope and budget under the chairmanship of eminent and influential public figures such as Keynes and Arnold Goodman. In the 1960s further radical developments took place. In the 1964-1966 Wilson Government Jennie Lee was appointed the first Minister for the Arts, an indication of the rise in status of the arts since the Second World War. The arts were no longer merely pencilled in. They were now incorporated into the governmental process.

The unleashing of new social forces in the 1960s was reflected in the world of art by the provision of 'fringe' and 'alternative' theatre for those wanting either a more radical and politically committed theatre or more permanent small-scale theatrical institutions than local amateur theatre companies. Conflict became more overt: the censorship laws were challenged by such cases as the publication of the unexpurgated version of D. H. Lawrence's *Lady Chatterley's Lover* and the Royal Court's attempt to get around the Lord Chamberlain's rules on theatre censorship. In this radical period the Arts Council tried to accommodate the energies of younger, less-established artists by creating its new, but vaguely titled, 'New Activities Sub-committee', half of the members of which were to be young people. Despite this, the Arts Council seemed unable to respond to new trends in any way other than with vague promises to incorporate the 'new' and the 'young'. The sub-committee was later renamed the 'Arts and Community Committee'.

Also during the 1960s and 1970s the debate about the separation of art and politics re-emerged. Institutionalised beliefs about the division between art and politics were challenged by those who argued, on the one hand, that all art was political, and on the other that all life was art, including a pile of bricks.

Two ideological strands ran through the 1960s art world. The first was to be found amongst the fringe radical element who sought funding but resisted authority; the second amongst those who felt that the arts were now part of the Welfare State. Citizens now had a democratic right of access to subsidised art. The corporatist style of intervention in the world of funded arts reached its zenith under Arnold Goodman. In the 1969 Annual Report of the Arts Council he wrote:

'Within our society there is now a widespread feeling that the provision of drama and music and painting and all culture in its broadest sense is no longer to be regarded as a privilege for a few, but is the democratic right of the entire community.'

The attempt to incorporate the more radical and anarchistic elements into the public-funded world of the Arts Council met with some resistance. Bryan Appleyard explains:

'The idea of the New Activities Sub-committee was a response to this explosion of the 'fringe' in the 1960s. The Arts Council's response was to say: "We respond to creativity as and when it occurs, we don't try and direct it." They didn't quite realise what they were taking on, both in financial commitments and in aesthetic terms. The New Activities Sub-committee, which took in various people from these new activities, failed because of the intrinsic anarchy in these activities. Even a Labour Government and a left-wing Arts Council couldn't answer the sorts of challenges that were being put up by extreme groups because it was in their nature to be anarchistic and rebellious. The consensus which had led to the refunding of the arts in 1945 no longer existed. There were some external political factors, the Vietnam War and things like that, which made these people simply resist organising.'

In the meantime, money was flowing in and big prestige projects were undertaken with government support. The National Theatre, the Hayward Gallery, the National Film Theatre and the Queen Elizabeth Hall completed the arts complex on the South Bank that had begun with the Royal Festival Hall in 1951.

In the 1970s funds still flowed but there was increasing concern about the level of subsidies being allotted – public finance in all areas of state activity began to be scrutinised. Commercial sponsorship emerged slowly as an alternate source of funding, a development very much in accord with the thinking of the 1979 Government under Margaret Thatcher. The rapid growth of the Arts Council's spending power under Arnold Goodman's chairmanship meant that questions about the relative value of the arts would inevitably be raised. The realisation that 'art' was rather a difficult term to define academically led the politically shrewd operators in the arts to redefine the arts as part of the 'heritage and tourist industry', and a big earner for the British economy. Bryan Appleyard:

> 'It was suddenly perceived as a very large industry indeed. Government money going to the Arts Council is one thing, but its quite another when you think of the sort of ancilliary industries that are involved. If you take in publishing, broadcasting and so on then you're talking about big businesses. If you lump them together with leisure and entertainment you're talking of three thousand million pounds.'

The advent of the monetarist Government of Margaret Thatcher presented a threat to the Arts Council. Bryan Appleyard explains the background in *The Culture Club*:

> 'In waking up to the size and significance of the arts industry, the Government had also become alert to the fact that its prime means of intervention and involvement in that industry was via a somewhat eccentric organisation, which seemed to indulge itself in highly publicised rows with appalling regularity.'

In this context the role of the Arts Council was questioned in two reports. In 1982 the Select Committee on Education, Science and the Arts published the report of one of its sub-committees which was entitled *Public and Private Funding of the Arts*. Whilst stressing the importance of the arts and the provision of government subsidies, the report questioned the appropriateness of the Arts Council. It argued for the appointment of a minister of Cabinet rank to head a new Department of Arts, Heritage and Tourism.

Then, in 1983, the Government had to find extra funds for the Royal Shakespeare Company and the Royal Opera House. The Prime Minister asked Clive Priestley, who had been in the Prime Minister's Office, to examine the efficacy of these two organisations. Priestley's subsequent report looked favourably on the two organisations but recommended direct government funding of the Royal Shakespeare Company, the National Theatre, the Royal Opera House and the English National Opera, thus reducing the role of the Arts Council.

The Arts Council was portrayed as being ineffectively bureaucratic and prone to publicity-attracting rows. The Conservative-dominated Parliament and Government were therefore well placed to roll back the corporatist carpet of government intervention by ending the existence of the 39-year-old quango. Not working in the Arts Council's favour was its incompetent lobbying at a time when the Government's ideological antipathy to public spending by non-department bodies was at its height. Bryan Appleyard writes:

> '... A reluctance occasionally to abandon the particular has doomed the Culture Club to become a mass of opposing cliques whispering breathlessly to each other from sumptuously upholstered armchairs.'

By 1984 the Arts Council's existence was at stake and lobbying started in earnest. The numerous bodies dependent on subsidy knew they might be singled out for a cut in grant or, even worse, no subsidy at all. With the Arts Council's report on funding due to be made public on 30 March, the days between the publication of the Priestley report in January and the end of March were a frenetic period in the art world: petitions were signed, letters written to *The Times*, Council members and journalists lobbied.

In 1980 grants to 41 minor organisations had been cut, but in 1984 it was not just fringe bodies that faced the axe. Possible casualties included the Hayward Art Gallery, which cost £500 000 a year to run, the Serpentine Gallery, costing £80 000, the Royal Court Theatre and one London orchestra out of the big four: the London Symphony Orchestra, the Royal Philharmonic, the London Philharmonic and the Philharmonia.

'Must the Arts Die?' was the heading of a large advertisement placed in *The Times* by the National Committee for the Campaign to Assist the Arts in the week following the Arts Council report. And this note of doom was sounded frequently throughout the early months of 1984. The Royal Court enlisted the support of a host of notables from the world of drama. The correspondence pages of *The Times* throughout the month of March resounded with famous names. Had *The Times* been paying for this array of talent they would undoubtedly have had to reduce the value of the

prize money they were offering in their promotional
'portfolio' game which was introduced that year. Letters
arrived from Alan Ayckbourn, Alan Bennett, Tom
Stoppard, David Storey and Arnold Wesker.

Later that month Peter Hall of the National Theatre and
Terry Hands and Trevor Nunn of the Royal Shakespeare
Company wrote in defence of the Royal Court. The week
before publication of the report *The Times* received a collective letter from Sir Hugh Willatt, Richard Hoggart and
others, all of whom had been associated with the Arts
Council's Drama Advisory Panel, extolling the virtues of the
Royal Court and praising its record as the theatre which
'since 1955 has always been considered a national theatre
for new writing.' The luminaries continued:

> '[Arts Council members] will surely not wish to treat
> any of its advisory panels or its own departmental
> officers with the contempt which a decision to cripple
> the English Stage Company (at the Royal Court)
> would unmistakeably signal.'

A further threat to the arts at this time stemmed from the
Government's intention to abolish the metropolitan
authorities, such as the GLC, which had traditionally also
subsidised the arts. On 1 March 1984 the GLC placed a
full-page advertisement in *The Times* headed 'The Arts in
Danger' which was signed by 131 leading figures of the
British art establishment, including Robert Bolt, Melvyn
Bragg, Peter Brook, Sir Hugh Casson, Sir John Gielgud, Sir
Charles Groves, Joseph Losey, Lord Miles, Henry Moore,
John Mortimer, Sir Claus Moser, Lord Olivier, Joan Plow-
right, Brian Rix, Ken Russell, Ronnie Scott, Ned Sherrin,
Sir Michael Tippett and Michael Winner (see page 91).

When the Arts Council's intentions were finally revealed
the storm had practically blown itself out. The Hayward
and Serpentine Galleries and the Royal Court survived; one
of the four London orchestras, as yet unspecified, was to be
cut back or moved to the provinces; 15 theatre companies,
such as the King's Head, Islington and the Yvonne Arnaud
Theatre at Guildford, had their grants withdrawn: Opera 80
lost its grant; the literature subsidy was halved; and
although the total budget was cut by £5.5 million, £6 million
was removed from London and redistributed throughout the

provinces. Most sorely hit was the literature department with 50 per cent removed from a budget which was already less than one per cent of the total expenditure of the Arts Council. This cut, from £900 000 to £450 000, led to the resignation of three of 12 advisers on the literature panel.

In Bryan Appleyard's view the cuts in, and redistribution of, the budget was less significant, despite the public nature of the lobbying, than the fact that the Arts Council was still alive and kicking.

'The key function of *The Glory of the Garden* was to save the Arts Council ... I think devolution to the regions was the top dressing, with the real sub-text concerned with making the Arts Council respectable in the Government's eyes.'

In the pages of *The Times*, where so much of the public lobbying had been in evidence, Bryan Appleyard wrote a re-appraisal of the Arts Council's lobbying abilities:

'In the details of the launch of the strategy the Council has displayed a new sophistication. The last time significant cuts were made the publicity effect was catastrophic. The wave of protest peaked after the announcement and the protesters thus had the last word. This time it was altogether different; by a process of controlled and highly artificial leaks the anguish was generated before the announcement.' (*The Times* 11.4.84)

5.2 *Lobbying for the arts*

The recent examination of the cost and financial efficiency of the arts has led to a re-evaluation of what the term encompasses. In *The Culture Club* Bryan Appleyard argues that the word 'art' has become redundant. Instead we should think of a number of 'arts industries' which have a turnover of between £3000 and £4000 million a year. More than a third of overseas tourists go to the theatre when in London and export earnings from the arts add up to £1000 million per annum. The view expounded by those who want to protect existing public subsidies is that the amount of public money spent is insignificant when compared with the vast amounts earned for the country's economy by the tourist and art industries. Protecting the arts in the 1980s has meant a departure from the beliefs of the Goodman days when art was represented as a 'democratic right of the entire community'. Now the arts are held to be a vital ingredient in the booming business of tourism and art exportation.

Whether to subsidise art, and how to do it, are the two questions which have been the main focus of parliamentary debates on the arts since 1945. A third view of the arts brought up in these debates is that it is an elitist pastime paid for by the public. As the Conservative MP David Maclean asked of the Under-Secretary of the Arts, William Waldegrave, in the House of Commons on 25 June 1984:

> 'For how long does he think the taxpayer can continue subsidising the Royal Opera House to the tune of £25 per ticket per performance?. How long are we taxpayers to be made to pay for the pleasures of the elitist few?

Two other Conservative MPS who have actively defended public subsidy of the arts are Patrick Cormack and Nicholas Fairbairn. As poet and artist and former member of the Edinburgh Festival Committee, Nicholas Fairbairn replies thus to such criticism:

> 'It's an absurd concept, it's like saying, "Why should we pay for the blind because only a minority of us are blind?" The arts are considered to be the highest form of human achievement and the taxpayer has got to pay for them to be able to take place. In any case it isn't the elitist few. The people, for instance, who go to the Edinburgh Festival are not dukes and duchesses. They are thousands of people from all walks of life who enjoy opera and music, and to regard it as elitist is just absolutely idiotic.... I mean, for all I know there's only one person in a million who ever uses a public lavatory, but there's no reason why the tax payer shouldn't have to pay for them.'

Patrick Cormack was Chairman of the inquiry into arts funding set up by the House of Commons Select Committee on Education, Science and Arts. In October 1982 it published its report, *Public and Private Funding of the Arts*, stressing the central position of arts in British life. The Government's reply in a white paper in January 1984 was to reject most of their recommendations. It did not propose to adopt the recommended aboliton or reduction of VAT on theatre tickets nor did it respond to the demand for a Ministry of Arts, Heritage and Tourism headed by a minister with a seat in the Cabinet. Patrick Cormack:

> 'It was a very good report ignored by Government. It was totally non-ideological. We had a Select Committee which ranged from the fairly far right to the fairly far left and it was the only report we produced in the 1979 Parliament which was totally unanimous. It was referred to in the press as being the most important inquiry Parliament had conducted into the arts, certainly since the war. I thought it very unfortunate that the Government took 18 months or so to reply to it, and when they replied to it it was in a very flimsy little document. It made a few flattering noises about the general quality of the report and then proceeded to dismiss it.'

Arguments about the economics of public subsidy, commercial sponsorship or market forces are bound up with questions about the relationship between the arts and politics. As we have seen, the Arts Council had originally been set up to provide some degree of independence from direct government interference. Patrick Cormack argues that questions concerning the arts should always be dealt with in a non-partisan atmosphere: 'They should not be kicked around by hack party politicians.' Bryan Appleyard, however, feels that this point of view would be difficult to maintain because of the differing ideological perspectives in the two main parties:

> 'Art on the Labour agenda occupies a quite different place from that on the Tory agenda. It changed from the era of technological optimism of Harold Wilson's period which was slightly different to the welfare optimism of the Attlee Government. Art was seen as an essential part of this. Now this is based on a rather optimistic view of culture which says: "If you put on art, people will go to the theatre and be improved by it." The problem is that art is wayward and difficult and often refuses to pander to those audiences and

often gets into all sorts of problems, which people find unpopular and unpleasant. You can't legislate for art. There is a contradiction in what seems to be the central welfare position of art. It never quite does what you want it to do. If the NHS puts a bandage on a wound it stops bleeding. You can't say that with art. You have this rather shifting, sometimes non-existent, thing. It makes it difficult for the Labour Party.

The Tories have been traditionally mistrustful of the arts because they tend to be very left-wing, particularly the fringe and small theatre groups. They have predominently left-wing sympathies. So, necessarily, the Tories have been more associated with big art like Covent Garden, the National Theatre and so on.'

The reality is that state subsidies attract the inevitability of state influence. Two extracts from the correspondence page of *The Times* in 1984 make this point:

'The decision by the Arts Council implies that there are political guidelines about the use of public money for promoting the arts. In view of this case, would it not be a good thing that the public be informed what these guidelines are, how and by whom they are applied, and what is their legal status?

From Prof. Alexander Goehr, University of Cambridge'

(1.3.84)

'How could it be other than that the distribution of money by the state and its agencies is influenced by political criteria? The state is a political organisation. State-funding of any activity, be it arts, science, or enterprise, thus inevitably means political influence over, if not control of, the activity.

From J. Burton'

(7.3.84)

How successful are the artists in lobbying within the political arena? Bryan Appleyard sees the 'reluctance to abandon the particular' and the 'mass of opposing cliques' as working against the arts lobby in general. Bryan Forbes identifies a similar problem in the film industry which he describes as 'fragmented':

'It is fragmented in terms of the number of craft unions that are involved, and also you've got the Cinematograph Society, the cinema owners, the distributors, the producers, the actors, three technicians' unions, and you have a very great number of splinter groups like the Guild of Film Editors, The Directors' Guild of Great Britain, the Writers' Guild, the Authors' Guild. You are talking about a great number of people, all of whom have a particular axe to grind and all of whom think their priorities are the ones that should be listened to.'

There are also a number of forceful and articulate celebrities in the arts lobby who are prepared to fight hard for their own particular area. 'Prima donnas', as Patrick Cormack calls them, like Roy Strong and Peter Hall, are inevitable. Bryan Appleyard refers to such people as 'the priesthood':

'I think, inevitably, if you subsidise the arts and if you have big arts organisations as we do, you create a priesthood, the sort of people who are entrusted with the public money to give us art. This is obviously a highly factional situation because some people are in and some people are out. The subsidised arts are deeply involved in relative levels of subsidy for different organisations. It's a constant irritation as to who's getting more and why one organisation gets more subsidy than another. It's because subsidy is just one form of income along with the box office and sponsorship.'

Whatever you call them, there is one advantage in being a public celebrity in the world of the arts – your chances of access to politicians improve. Mixing with the powerful is a game the famous play. At dinner at Chequers, Bryan Forbes was able to explain personally to the Prime Minister why he thought the 1984 budget proposals on capital allowances for films were a mistake. Neither does he seem to have had many difficulties in getting himself invited to lunch at No. 11 Downing Street:

'I have had meetings with various Chancellors over the years, usually on questions of the BBC licence fee which I've often championed as being too low. I think it's very good value for money even though a great number of people seem very reluctant to pay it every year.'

But how did he manage to arrange such meetings?

'I just wrote to them. I spoke to Tony Barber, and wrote to him. I had long meetings with Geoffrey Howe, when he was Chancellor. I also had a meeting with Denis Healey.'

Peter Hall's diaries show that he was also a regular visitor to the tables and homes of the political establishment:

'Wednesday 12 February 1975: To Buckingham Palace for the Queen's reception for the media . . . The Queen asked me when the National Theatre would open. I said I didn't know . . .'

'Thursday 8 April 1976: To No. 10 for dinner. Callaghan is a much more relaxed, genial and re-assuring host than Wilson, who is inclined to look embarrassed and slightly shifty, as if he were thinking about something else. The main object of the dinner was to promote British theatre in Iran . . .'

'Tuesday 6 September 1977: Worked at home. Then visited Arnold Goodman . . .'

'Tuesday 5 December 1978: To an *Observer* dinner at Lincoln's Inn. If the Establishment exists, it was there: Harold Macmillan, Henry Kissinger, Merlyn Rees, Harold Lever, newspaper editors, heads of television . . .'

'Wednesday 7 November 1979: Lunch with Norman St John Stevas. . . .'

'Politics is now a branch of show business' records Peter Hall in his diary for Christmas 1978 having just watched Harold Wilson on *The Morecambe and Wise Show*. A more likely explanation of this phenomena is that the world of the arts and show business need to keep the politicians on their side if they are to survive financially; they become adept at playing the courtier. Politicians need to keep in the public eye if they are to succeed. The successful on either side thrive on each other.

Undoubtedly the problem of funding has been foremost on the art lobbyists' agendas over the years, but the question of censorship has also vexed artist and politician. And when it comes to lobbying about the censorship of the theatre and television, then even Prime Ministers and royalty are likely to join in the debate, as this extract from *The Diaries of a Cabinet Minister* (Crossman, 1975–77) shows:

'Wednesday, 26 July, 1967: To Downing Street for morning prayers. The only subject the PM wanted to talk about was theatre censorship. There had just been published a report from a very representative committee which unanimously recommended the abolition of the functions of the Lord Chamberlain as censor of the living drama. This Roy Jenkins had very much wanted to accept but the PM told . . . me this would be a terrible mistake and he also let us know that he'd sent George Wigg to the Home Affairs Committee to warn them against accepting it. I had had to leave the Committee just when George Wigg was starting to speak and hadn't realised that he was the PM's emissary: indeed I thought he'd gone there with a brief from Arnold Goodman, who was a member of the original departmental committee. Harold [Wilson]'s explanation was very elaborate, I think because he was a little embarrassed. "I've received representations from the Palace", he said. "They don't want to ban all plays about live persons, but they want to make sure that there's somebody who'd stop the kind of play about Prince Philip which would be painful to the Queen. Of course," he hurriedly added, "they're not denying that there should be freedom to write satirical plays, take-offs, caricatures: what they want to be able to ban are plays devoted to character assassination and they mention, as an example, *Mrs Wilson's Diary*."

I pricked up my ears. *Mrs Wilson's Diary* is, of course, one of the most popular features of *Private Eye* and there were ideas about putting it on the stage. When I asked him, Harold told me that he had been shown the text of the play, which made him out a complete mugwump and gave a picture of George Brown's drinking and swearing and using four-letter words. My first reaction was to tell him that he could hardly keep censorship of the live theatre and leave television and radio free. He had a quick reply. "That'll all be lined up now," he said "because Charlie Hill has already cleaned up ITV and he'll do the same to BBC now I'm appointing him chairman." It was obvious from the way he talked that he wanted the censorship as much as the Queen. Indeed he wanted it so much that he'd put it on Thursday's Cabinet agenda.'

Politicians' concern with the standards of decency in the arts is not confined to Cabinet discussion. As former Chairman of the Scottish Society for the Defence of Literature, Nicholas Fairbairn QC defended and supported theatres and writers who were prosecuted under the censorship laws. The Scottish Society for the Defence of Literature had two objectives, one to lobby the Arts Council on behalf of writers and the other to defend writers from censorship. In the early '60s a number of books had been subjected to what the literary world regarded as artistic censorship and the prosecution saw as protecting public morals. Notorious cases involved *Lady Chatterley's Lover* and *Fanny Hill*. Fairbairn also acted for the defence when Anna Kessler was prosecuted for indecency. This stemmed from a poetry exhibition at the Edinburgh Festival where she was wheeled across the stage naked. Fairbairn argued in court, successfully, that 'the human form is not something of which one has to be ashamed. It has been the inspiration of artists through the ages.' Winning the case had an enormous effect on the general attitude towards the censorship of plays and books in Scotland.

As many of the controversies on funding and censorship could be guaranteed a considerable amount of media coverage, especially when it involved naked ladies or artistic personalities, then knowing how to make use of the media became a vital part in determining the success or failure of issues in this area. This realisation applies not only to other areas of lobbying, but to politics in general.

5.3 *Using the media*

In the early 1980s Julian Critchley, MP for Aldershot, the home of the British Army, was smuggled into the Admiralty disguised as an able-seaman by Sir Henry Leach, then the most senior naval officer in the Ministry of Defence. This subterfuge was not related to Critchley's position as an MP, nor even his undoubted knowledge of naval tactics, but to the fact that Critchley at that time wrote a regular column in the *Daily Telegraph*. The Navy was soliciting his support in those pre-Falkland days against cuts in the naval budget. The admirals, fearing the outcome would mean a smaller fleet, 'lobbied like mad' according to Critchley, against the proposals of the then Secretary of State for Defence, John Nott. They turned to any sympathetic journalist they could find.

To have media sympathetic to the campaign or cause of a lobby group is a powerful asset. As we have seen, the Arts Council under Sir William Rees-Mogg, a former editor of *The Times*, conducted a skilful lobby campaign against cuts in subsidies throughout the early part of 1984. By taking advantage of leaked information the Council was able to rally supporters for particular theatres, orchestras and galleries whilst appearing to be planning expenditure cuts likely to be approved of by a frugal-minded Government.

This style of lobbying is a good illustration of pre-emptive lobbying, that is, raising the issue publicly and defining it in such a way that opinion is swayed before final decisions have been made. In contrast to this was the campaign mounted by the hot-food operators in protest at the imposition of VAT on take-away food introduced by the 1984 budget. Their petition of 600 000 signatures came too late – the decisions had already been taken. The Hot Food Take-away Action Group will now have to conduct a protracted and persistent campaign if it is to get the policy reversed.

In general, as Bryan Appleyard points out, the media are favourably disposed towards the arts:

> 'The arts have a lot of inbuilt sympathy in the media. You can very easily stir up sympathy for saving a theatre. The reaction of the press is to be in sympathy with creative people. The exceptions to that are where you get the sort of Tate Gallery brick story where you get a should-we-be-spending-money-on-this-rubbish story.'

Peter Hall also detects media sympathy for the arts, especially amongst the quality papers. On 19 July 1978 he attended a one-day Council of the Arts organised by the Conservative Party. The conference didn't achieve anything

but he reflected in his diary as to why the then Shadow
Spokesman on Science and the Arts had arranged it:

> 'I think a reason for this conference is that Norman St
> John Stevas may have caught on to something which I
> am surprised the political parties didn't realise long
> ago: there are certainly no votes in the arts, but there is
> considerable media sympathy. Any party that
> promises money for the arts is liable to be treated sym-
> pathetically by heavyweight journalists. It might even
> cause the *Guardian* to smile at the Tory Party, however
> coolly.'

For a lobbyist, having the media on your side is obviously an
asset, but what do we mean by the 'media' and what is its
significance for the process of lobbying?

The media is the collective term that refers to the various
institutions through which information and messages are
disseminated. Accepted usage means that we are talking
about the 'mass media', that is, those directed towards large
audiences. The media is not a single institution and the
variations between the differing media, e.g. press and television, are as important to understand as are the differences
in style within a medium like the press, e.g. the *Sun* and the
Guardian. In the political context radio, television and newspapers are more relevant than books, cinema and records.

Their major political significance is that in a large,
socially heterogeneous nation like the UK they permit the
existence of a nationwide agenda of political debate. One
side-effect of this state of affairs is that the debate is highly
selective and the dialogue very much a one-way flow of
information from those who control the media to those who
receive its messages.

Since the 1950s television has become the dominant
political medium during general elections. Harold Macmillan, Prime Minister from 1957 to 1963, was the first
leading politician in the UK to exploit the use of the television, although he bemoaned the decline in oratory which
has accompanied the shift from public meetings to television politics. He told Ludovic Kennedy in an interview on
BBC Television just after the 1983 General Election: 'the art
of speaking, which is a very difficult art, [is] now almost
gone. For instance, take the last election, it was almost

entirely fought on television.' (Quoted in Max Atkinson's book *Our Masters' Voices* (1984).)

Today live oratory is a less important political skill than televisuality. The 1983 election campaign, according to Atkinson, saw two party leaders–Michael Foot of the Labour Party and Roy Jenkins of the SDP – who didn't possess television appeal. Both are more adept at public speaking, whether in the Chamber of the House of Commons or at public meetings. Confronting them was Margaret Thatcher who had been well groomed to look and sound good on television – teeth capped, hair immaculate, voice trained to sound less shrill and more authoritative.

For lobbyists the media can be crucial if the purpose of a campaign is to mobilise public support. Knowing how to manipulate the media becomes one of the necessary skills of the lobby group.

There are three functions that the media can fulfil for a lobby organisation:

1   a means of acquiring information;
2   a deliberative forum;
3   a means of exerting influence.

Being an effective operator in the public arena requires that current topical issues in the media are known about, and responded to, when they are relevant to your lobby interest. Lobbyists scan the papers, or if they are wealthy enough hire public relations firms to do it for them, in the search for stories, data, opinions and letters related to themselves. Mary Whitehouse reveals in her diary that reading a newspaper led to one of her famous initiatives:

> '24 October 1980. Saw in today's *Daily Telegraph* that the Attorney-General was sending a lawyer to see *The Romans in Britain* tonight. Ernest [her husband] said, "Why don't we do the same?"' (Whitehouse, *A Most Dangerous Woman?*, 1982)

Des Wilson explains how the letter pages of the newspapers are a potential source of recruitment for his campaigns:

> 'Nine out of 10 letters that appear in the *Guardian* or *The Times* on issues that we have originated, or are involved in, come from people we have never heard of. What we do do is keep in touch with the people who write them, saying: "Hey, great letter that, why don't you get

involved in our campaign?" So actually the letters are a source of new recruits and supporters for us.'

The second function of the media for a lobby group is deliberative, in that beliefs and stances can be clearly and publicly declared and clarified. We have noted how the correspondence pages of *The Times* became a forum for public figures to voice their support for threatened companies and theatres in 1984. Bryan Forbes has often written to the papers on topics as varied as the National Youth Theatre and the BBC licence fee. He 'automatically' chooses *The Times* in the first instance because it is today's equivalent of the 'village pump' – the place to hear the latest gossip and initiate your own.

The Times is also a good place to make authoritative statements declaring or clarifying your point of view, as Peter Hall's diaries reveal:

'Saturday 9 December 1972 ... A brief chat to Trevor [Nunn of the Royal Shakespeare Company]. Norman St John Stevas [Minister for the Arts 1979–81, 1973–4] has told him he is worried about the Angus Maude business and the left-wing, right-wing nonsense which has continued in the papers all week. [Conservative MP Angus Maude had resigned as a Governor of the RSC because a letter to *The Times* from Trevor Nunn declared the RSC was 'basically a left-wing organisation'.] He warned Trevor that a question will be asked in the House – an ugly question. He urged Trevor to make his position clear by another letter to *The Times*.'

Another, more dramatic way of achieving media publicity for a cause is by 'leaking' information. The *Guardian* has been the beneficiary of recent leaks about cruise missiles from a Ministry of Defence employee, Sarah Tisdall, who was later imprisoned. The *Daily Telegraph* also has had its moments, as is pointed out in Stephen Koss's book *The Rise and Fall of the Political Press* (1984). Koss notes that in 1936 it was the *Daily Telegraph* rather than *The Times* which was kept fully informed by Prime Minister Stanley Baldwin about the developments in the crisis that culminated in the abdication of King Edward VIII.

The third function of the media is to act as an influence over public debate and opinion. To achieve influence a lobby group must understand how the press, television and radio sway public debate. The media's political significance stems from its ability to influence the agenda of public debate, determine who takes part, set the narrative contours of the debate and, sometimes, fix its outcome (for it is not clear to what extent the media reflects or creates 'public opinion').

The agenda is as important for what it excludes as for what it includes. The political agenda as covered by the media has a ritualised quality to some extent in that predictable coverage will be given to key events in the political calendar, e.g. the Queen's Speech at the Opening of the Parliamentary Session, Budget day, the party conferences. But the issues selected for coverage will vary depending on factors such as recent political context. The 1983 Conservative Party conference at Blackpool will be remembered for its focus on the question of whether Cecil Parkinson would resign from the Cabinet because of a revelation about his love life with his secretary.

The ability to exclude an issue from public debate by stealth or censorship is a powerful weapon in a democracy. The ability to exclude individuals or groups is another. Mary Whitehouse, for example, feels aggrieved not so much that some of the issues she supports are debarred from a public hearing by the media, but that she herself is. When her 'Clean Up TV' campaign began to get off the ground in the early part of 1964, two things, she feels, developed:

> 'On the one hand I was banned on BBC Television for 11 years, literally, nobody in BBC Television must speak to me or come anywhere near me and they must not have me on any programme. At the same time there was hardly a week-end when there wasn't some snide remark, or even the series *Swizzlewick* [1966 comedy series], which I don't suppose people remember these days, but that's how the series *Swizzlewick* was built, it was based on our campaign.'

Larry Gostin feels that the agenda of political items in the media is very stereotyped:

> 'If you look at the media's interest in Parliament, it will follow a very consistent pattern. Every television news viewer will know that it begins with economics and the

Treasury and the current interest rates and then it goes to foreign affairs, then it moves to trades unions and standard labour relations activities. Ten years ago, in particular, you would have heard very little about the environment, freedom of information, mental patients' rights, civil rights, anti-discrimination on a whole range of areas like the rights of women, gay people, black people.'

If enough one-sided news and information is regularly printed and broadcast then clearly the political outlook of the public will be fixed into the acceptance of a particular view. But knowing what the political significance of the media is and how its influence can be exerted is not to explain why it should act in such a way.

The reasons for the media's role in the shaping and fixing of political dialogue are varied but include: the partisanship of media proprietors, commercial considerations, technical factors, editorial policy and government influence.

It is in the newspapers that the proprietor's bias and personal whims can most easily be detected. The deliberate manipulation of the news in the pages of the newspapers owned by men like Northcliffe, Rothermere, Beaverbrook and Murdoch are well chronicled. The willingness to espouse particular causes and focus public attention on others was a powerful weapon in their hands.

Beaverbrook made no attempt to hide his political views in *Daily Express* headlines and editorials. Lord Rothermere in the 1930s supported the Mosley fascists and their anti-semitic activities by donating secret funds. More recently BOSS, the South African secret service, realising the value of having sympathetic journalistic coverage in Western countries, planned to gain control of the *Observer* by attempting to buy it. The plan failed.

It is the more radical lobby groups and political parties who complain most vociferously about the conservative bias in most of the national dailies except the *Guardian, Daily Mirror* and the *Morning Star*. 'A landslide by deception' is how Michael Foot described the media's role in the 1983 General Election (*Newsnight* BBC 2, 4.10.83). In his last speech as leader of the Labour Party at the annual party conference in Brighton 1983 he revived memories of the forged Zinoviev letter published by the *Daily Mail* in 1924, an attempt to discredit the emergent Labour Party during the election by associating it with the Bolsheviks in Russia.

He spoke vehemently against the press and told the delegates:

> 'During the election and at other periods the British people got a distorted and completely jaundiced picture of what was really happening ... I do not say it is all due to the arrival of Mr Murdoch in Britain. Although I think he bears his fair share, to say that would not be fair to others, would it? It would not be fair to our own old friend, the *Daily Mail*, the forger's gazette.'

Commercial considerations also affect the media's interest in lobby politics. To be financially viable newspapers have to attract both readers and advertisers. Television channels vie for audience ratings and news programmes are not immune from this constraint. Attracting as large as possible a readership or audience, of the right type, without alienating those who purchase advertising space can be a tricky road to tread.

Complicated issues which lack the essential of newsworthiness will not get media coverage. A newsworthy story is one which has some of the following elements: drama, novelty, controversy, and immediacy, and should be capable of being portrayed in a concrete way and by personalities, preferably celebrities. Television news is less obviously biased than that of the newspapers, but a lobby group's efforts to get media coverage must nevertheless fit into the editorial assumptions about newsworthiness, and be able to answer the question: what is the picture we can use and how can we give the story human interest?

Another constraint is how not to upset the advertisers whose expenditure might be crucial to the profitability of the paper or television or radio company. Mike Daube explains:

> 'There are some well documented cases of the tobacco lobby simply being able to swing the media as it wants. Just look around you. How many major British newspapers have run any kind of consistent campaign on cigarette smoking? Bearing in mind it kills 100,000

people prematurely each year and causes a loss to industry of more than 10 times as many working days as
strikes, why aren't the media taking it up? Where are
our campaigning journalists? And the answer is the
media aren't taking it up because of the sheer power of
tobacco advertising which is so important to them.

I remember when I was writing a piece on smoking
for the *Guardian*, I had a 'phone call from their advertising department and the chap said; "You won't be too
hard on low-tar cigarettes will you, I want to get some
advertising for Silk Cut."'

With their massive advertising expenditure the tobacco
companies are able to bring pressure to bear on the content
of newspapers. This led to a row at the *Sunday Times*, which
in 1980/81 had taken nearly £750000 worth of cigarette
advertising, according to Peter Taylor in *Smoke Ring*
(1984). Oliver Gillie, the medical correspondent, although
free to criticise cigarette smoking and advertising, was not
able to run a major campaign.

When it comes to 'news manipulation' then lobby groups
will be envious of the ability of the Government to fix the
news. Not only is central government a big spender in
advertising terms, but it is a major source of news information. Not to be invited to get the latest briefing from a
department or ministerial statement puts a reporter at a
disadvantage in the competitive world of journalists. The
'press lobby' at Westminster has been accused of working
too closely with government spokesmen. In their book *Sources Close to the Prime Minister* (1984), Michael Cockerell,
Peter Hennessey and David Walker document how governments fix the press lobby and use the Official Secrets Act to
their advantage. American political journalist, Andrew
Roth, who has worked in Westminster since 1950, also con-
firms this view of a 'press lobby', which, in exchange for
being kept 'in the know' does not reveal all to its readers.
In 1963 he was the first to release the story in his weekly
newsletter about the scandal involving War Minister John
Profumo's sexual involvement with prostitute Christine
Keeler who was also a friend of a Russian diplomat. Other
journalists knew about the story but their newspapers were
not willing to print it.

The tacit agreements between journalists and government not to rock the boat is mirrored by the attitudes of those lobby groups that are already in an influential position. Some prefer to maintain a low profile, eschew media publicity and operate behind the scenes. 'Rattling the sabre' in the media, ex-MP David Myles suggests, is sometimes done to convince the membership of a lobby group that something is happening when a decision has already been lost in private.

Some lobby groups have a long history of preferring the low-key approach of quiet influence. The CPRE has had a good deal of media coverage in the 1980s because of the number of issues it has been involved in, e.g. the Wildlife and Countryside Act, green-belt planning, and so on. But under the influence of Sir Herbert Griffin, Secretary for the CPRE from 1926 where it was founded and named the Council for the *Preservation*, rather than, as it now is, *Protection*, of Rural England, influence was sought until his retirement in the mid-1960s with the minimum of fuss.

The events of the 1980s has led the CPRE to adopt a higher media profile, but the Chairman, David Astor insists that it will not resort to media stunts to attract attention. Instead it will continue to put what he refers to as 'reasoned argument' to the relevant government departments. 'Going public' with an issue might jeopardise a group's relationship with Whitehall officials who have traditionally avoided the limelight and the possibility of more intense public and parliamentary scrutiny.

Typical of some of the more radical groups who dislike and disapprove of the idea of such image-management is the Abortion Law Reform Association. Its co-ordinator, Hilary Jackson, believes that credibility and not image should be the main concern:

'I think we have credibility ... and what matters most is women's own self-image, how they see themselves and how they relate to what they can and can't do with their lives. So how other people see us is in someways not our problem.'

Other lobbyists take a more active role in seeking to shape the public's perception of themselves by using modern advertising techniques to ensure not only that the message gets across, but does so in such a way as to generate a sympathetic public image. Press secretaries can be appointed, public relations specialists hired and advertising campaigns used to market a 'cause' or 'interest' in the same way that companies seek to sell products. Greenpeace has taken to renting advertising hoarding space to dissuade people from buying fur coats with the slogan:

> 'It takes 40 dumb animals to make a fur coat – but only one to wear it.'

On a grander scale the GLC is spending £3 million a year on publicity material such as pamphlets and posters on commercial hoardings, and before the campaign to 'Save the GLC' is finished it is expected to spend £10 million of ratepayers' money. British Telecom, in an effort to create a favourable image amongst potential shareholders with privatisation imminent, spent £24·5 million in 1983 on advertising to convince us, the public, with our own money that it is one of the world leaders in information technology.

However, most lobby groups do not have this sort of money and rely instead on their access to, and knowledge of, the world of 'news-manufacturing' to feed information to the media with no cost to themselves. Making use of 'newsworthy' stories is one device if confrontation and drama is involved. Some groups, like Friends of the Earth, have become skilful at giving their rallies a newsworthy edge by the use of photogenic stunts, e.g. bottles returned in their thousands to Schweppes Ltd, inflatable whales, the use of animal costumes, and organising thousands of cyclists to descend *en masse* on Trafalgar Square.

Skilful campaigners know how to use their knowledge of media deadlines to exploit TV and press journalists' rivalry to be first with the news and how to word a succinct and interesting press release through which the working journalist can glean the basic facts for a news story without having to wade through reams of print. They also know which of the less well-off news-sheets, weeklies, local and trade papers would be delighted to be able to make use of a prepared story by just making a few amendments to the copy received.

Contacts are also essential. In 1977, Frank Field, then director of the CPAG, received leaked information about a

Cabinet discussion concerning the possibility of postponing the child benefit scheme – a social policy reform which the CPAG had originally fought hard for. It had been included in the Labour Party's manifesto of 1974 and subsequently they won the election. Field mobilised support from the Labour movement, Parliament and the public by an anonymous article printed in *New Society*. The intervention worked and the Cabinet bowed to the wishes of the aroused parties. To be effective as a lobbyist you have to be able, firstly, to respond quickly to events. This is helped if you have good contacts in the Government, preferably at all levels up to the Cabinet. Secondly you must be on good terms with editors, such as Paul Barker of *New Society*, to ensure that your story has an appropriate outlet.

However it is achieved, a benign media image is advantageous to a lobby group and can help shape public, parliamentary and government responses to a specific issue. A negative image, on the other hand, can be very damaging, as the Law Society discovered in 1984. The image of solicitors put across by the media during this year led Christopher Hewetson, President of the Law Society, to write a circular letter to all solicitors' firms in England and Wales stating that the solicitors' case to the public on the conveyancing monopoly had been frustrated by 'a hostile press'.

In fact it was not only the newspapers that had focussed in on the problems of the profession that year. In 1983/4 BBC Television's series *Out of Court* ran several stories about the problems of the profession, including the conveyancing monopoly, the question of advertising, and the complaints procedure. The profession, at a time when many solicitors' offices were being revolutionised by new computer technology, were annoyed by the media's willingness to repeat such accusations as that of David Tench of the Consumers' Association that: 'Solicitors are still using quill-pen procedure in the age of the computer.' Image and reality are not always the same.

Furthermore, images can be self-perpetuating and persistent. Individuals, once labelled with a particular reputation, find it hard to re-negotiate their public self, as Peter Hall discovered:

'Tuesday 20 January 1974: Early morning start. Then

> Sally Beauman arrived to interview me for the *Telegraph* colour mag. All the usual questions: "You have a reputation for being ruthless ..." "You like power ..." "Why do you work so hard ...?"
>
> She had been right through my cuttings in the Press Association library. She said I had one of the fattest files there.
>
> These files are self-perpetuating. I was described as being ruthless and power-loving by Peter Lewis in *Nova* magazine in about 1962. I have been ruthless and power-loving ever since.' (*Peter Hall's Diaries*, 1984)

Some lobby groups, unlike the Law Society, are not unhappy with their media stereotype. Some radical pro-abortion groups do not mind that the specific issue of abortion has been subsumed under the more general cause of womens' rights. The anti-abortion groups seem content with their more general image as the guardians of public morality. Julian Critchley, talking about the abortion lobbyists, commented with the generalisation:

> 'One is faced on the one hand with *Guardian* women saying that their wombs are their own, and on the other by nuns who put forward the case about the sanctity of life.'

The translation of the issue for a specific proposal, e.g. reducing the conditions under which abortion is available, to a more general debate between two stereotyped positions on womens' rights and religious conviction is not untypical of the history of many lobby-group conflicts. The future of the coal industry in 1984 was re-interpreted by the popular press into the issue of whether Britain is to live by the Rule of Law or under a Marxist tyranny led by Arthur Scargill.

In part this is a result of media stereotyping and simplification, and press bias, but it is also a feature of social and political issues that they become polarised around symbolic issues. A specific political issue comes to symbolise a broader social conflict about life-styles, class identification and moral values. It is not unknown for political postures to be adopted not on the basis of arguments and facts, but on the basis of the credibility, loyalty or legitimacy of an individual or group. It is not always the instrumental impact of a lobby group's proposal that is at stake in politics.

Joseph Gusfield's *Symbolic Crusade* (1963), a study of the lobbying by the Temperance movement at the beginning of the twentieth century which led to the Prohibition era in the USA, reveals that more than the simple instrumental prevention of alcohol consumption lay behind the mobilisation of public opinion. It was, he argues, an issue which highlighted significant differences in cultural outlook between, on the one hand, the predominantly poorer, recently arrived Catholic immigrants who settled in the cities, and on the other, the settled, affluent, Protestant, middle-class and rural Americans.

Gusfield sees this conflict in terms of 'status politics', or the struggle to have one group's cultural values embodied in law, signifying the prestige and honour of that group whilst denigrating those whose way of life is rejected by the law. He writes:

> 'Victory or defeat were consequently symbolic of the status and power of the cultures opposing each other.'

The symbolic aspect of law does not depend on engagement for its effect:

> 'The symbolic act invites consideration rather than overt reaction . . . Even if the law is broken, it was clear whose law it was.'

In both instrumental and symbolic clashes between lobby groups, the media has come to play an increasingly vital role in the way that political issues are raised and represented before the public. But the media is not immutable. An understanding of its logic and nature leads to an appreciation that well researched and controversial stories are two essential ingredients for serious journalism, thus providing an opportunity for a lobby group to influence its media image with well placed and well tried press releases. The point is not to bemoan one's media image, but to change it.

5.4 *Pluralist politics: a caveat*

The research material for this book came predominantly from interviews with successful lobbyists. The choice of political celebrities from the world of lobbying was not accidental. They have a collective experience which makes illuminating reading for those trying to understand or use the lobby system. One consequence of this, however, has been that the bulk of the material tells the story of prominent successes in lobby politics and how they were achieved through the institutional world of Parliament, party, government, EEC, the courts and the media.

Obviously there are also lobby victories which go unnoticed because secrecy was vital to their success. Many failures too go unrecorded because publicity would harm the reputation of those involved; and there are plenty of initiatives, of course, which end in compromise. Politics, after all, is not a science of the inevitable, but an 'art of the possible', in most lobbyists' view, a view which rejects fatalism and the idea that there can be foreordained or pre-destined determinants of political events. This is not to suggest that political actors operate with unlimited free will. They exist, as we all do, in a world which is not of our making. But nevertheless we have the choice of responding in various ways to constraints imposed by political institutions, cultural values and the social structure.

Structural realities of life, such as social class, ration the opportunities for action unevenly throughout society. Our cultural outlooks, formed by our upbringing and education, give us many of our taken-for-granted prejudices. These institutional, structural and cultural factors are prone to reification: that is, they take on an object-like, external quality which makes them seem barriers to action whereas they are in fact of human origin and capable of change. Furthermore, political events do not operate within a closed system. The context of world events and current affairs defies predictability. Events, conflicts and contingencies such as the Falkland War of 1982 and the coal dispute of 1984 will inevitably have unforeseen consequences for British politics. The real 'art of lobbying' is to understand the nature of these constraints and to know when to take advantage of contingent political episodes.

Even so there are those who subscribe to the 'what's the point of bothering' school of thought. They cite perhaps class domination, elite rule, media bias or government determination as the sources of their despair and cynicism. One consequence of this view is that it becomes a self-fulfilling prophecy. Withdrawing from a conflict will only have one possible outcome – your opponents win. Staying to fight for a cause at least means logically that you have not lost before the struggle has started. A belief in the ability to influence events is in many respects a cornerstone of the democratic system.

In 1983 and 1984 Ken Livingstone toured the country, speaking at fringe meetings at the party political conferences in an attempt to 'Save the GLC' despite the Conservative Government's obvious intention and manifesto promise to abolish it. I asked him whether this activity wasn't a waste of time. Ken Livingstone:

> 'I don't think that is the case. The Government can make up its mind, but people retain a freedom to try and change it and I think that we have a 50:50 chance of saving the GLC. No-one a year ago would have thought we would have been able to derail the Government's paving bill, which would have allowed [it] to take control of the GLC without elections. That was the most severe defeat a Conservative Government has suffered in the House of Lords this century, and it was caused by the effort that we have put in. You can't neglect any one part of the British system in doing that; you have got to do your advertising, your public meetings, your petitions and, at the same time, your lobbying of key decision-makers.'

In Chapter 2 I looked at three theories of power which concede that lobbyists can influence political decisions. The first was pluralism which attributes to lobbyists the ability to bring about political change and sees this possibility as desirable. Pluralists see power as fluid, rather than fixed and concentrated in one place. Policy is open to negotiation because government is responsive to the pressure of public opinion and argument, if organised effectively. The Burkean view of politics, like that of the pluralists, also sees lobbying as being effective, but it tends to be more suspicious of its potential to do damage. Sectional interests, in misrepresenting or overstating their case, can distort Parliament's perception of the 'national interest'. The corporatists argue that lobbyists can affect policy change only if they infiltrate the governmental process and become incorporated into the consultative and decision-making bodies of central government. All three views are premised on the assumption that Britain is a democracy and that 'the people' have some influence over the decisions of government, or, in the Burkean view, at least over the selection of those who are to govern.

There are alternative political theories which deny the influence, or at least the democratic value, of political lobbying, and conclude that the practice is irrelevant or, at best, only of marginal political significance. Two such theories are elitism and Marxism.

Elite theories state that the political system is dominated by a small, select group into whose hands power is concentrated. In Britain the following are usually identified as the ruling elite: Cabinet members, top civil servants like Permanent Secretaries, public officials such as judges, heads of the professions, military chiefs of staff, financiers, industrialists and aristocrats, who by background, schooling and interest in maintaining the *status quo* come to share a common world-view which dictates their responses to political events. Hence lobbyists outside the ranks of the elite can only achieve success if sponsored by a member of the elite.

The Marxist approach is more sophisticated and challenges the relevance of pluralist assumptions on a number of levels. Firstly, Marxists do not accept that the political system is open to all sectional interests. They argue that because of the nature of class domination political competition is unequal. For instance, articulating a common class interest, and the ability to disseminate and legitimate that interest as the 'national interest' is much easier for the dominant economic class of bankers, financiers, industrialists and property holders than for workers and peasants.

Another fundamental assumption challenged by this class-view of society is that political institutions do not dominate society. Power is located in economic institutions and the corresponding economic relationships of property ownership and control. The banks are more powerful than Parliament, and share-dealing more vital than vote-counting. Reforms in the political sphere are at most marginal concessions. For a Marxist the facts of economic life provide the key to understanding what it is that determines the basic relationships in society rather than religious, political, sexual or legal institutions. In reply to the historical argument that religion seemed to dominate life in medieval Europe and politics in the Greek and Roman city-states, Marx said in *Das Kapital*:

> 'This much is clear, that the Middle Ages could not live on Catholicism, nor the ancient world on politics ... on the contrary, it is the mode in which they gained a livelihood that explains why in one case politics, and in the other Catholicism, played a chief part ... Don Quixote long ago paid the penalty for wrongly imagining that knight errantry was compatible with all economic forms of production.'

The logic of Marxism leads to a denigration of the role of political action other than that addressed to the overthrow of the system of class relationships. In Ralph Miliband's essay 'Political Action, Determinism, and Contingency' (Miliband, *Political Power and Social Theory*, 1980) he makes a distinction between 'generational history', in which political action and actors effect social change in the short run, and 'transgenerational history', in which, over a longer period and with the exception of nuclear war, class realities prevail and with them the various manifestations of economic exploitation, political oppression and social alienation.

A Marxist would regard the political reforms achieved by lobbyists, such as Michael Young and Des Wilson, as at best the marginal but inconsequential victories of bourgeois individualists, and, at worst, a means of political distraction from the real struggle at hand.

To conclude, there are those who through cynicism, fatalism, or alienation share a common attitude that lobbying is not worth bothering about. There are others who share a common theoretical view about the inappropriateness of lobbying and therefore seek other means of achieving political goals.

In the Introduction I stated that this book was not envisaged as a comprehensive study of all forms of power or of all means of persuasion. Instead it has focused on those activities which have sought via the process of lobbying to influence the policy decisions of central government.

For those engaged in politics, whether they choose to operate within or outside the existing political system, there is still the moral question of how far should they pursue their objectives regardless of the consequences for others. There are those who eschew the ballot box and lobbying as a means of seeking to influence political decisions. The Animal Liberation Front justifies direct action, even when illegal, on the grounds that although vivisection is legal it is not moral. There are others whose actions are justified primarily by political ends rather than moral considerations. During the week of the 1984 Annual Conservative Party Conference a bomb exploded which killed five people staying at the Grand Hotel, Brighton. In that same week when the bishops of the Church of England had been scolded for their remarks about the miners' strike and accused by conference delegates of bringing religion and morality into politics, the bomb was a forceful reminder of what can happen when morality is left out and political ends are pursued regardless of means.

Booklist

ALDERMAN, G. *Pressure groups and government in Great Britain* Longman, 1984

APPLEYARD, B. *The culture club: crisis in the arts* Faber, 1984

ATKINSON, M. *Our masters' voices* Methuen, 1984

BAGEHOT, W. *The English constitution* intro. R. H. S. Crossman, Fontana, 1963

BRITTAN, S. *The role and limits of government* Temple Smith, 1983

BROTHERTON, I. *Ministerial appointments to National Parks* Council for National Parks, 1983

BRYCE, J. *American commonwealth* 3 vols Macmillan, 1888 op

BRYCE, J. *Modern democracies* Macmillan, 1921 op

BURKE, E. *Works* Vol III Thomas M'Lean, 1823 op

CHRISTOPH, J. B. *Capital punishment and British politics* Allen and Unwin, 1962 op

COCKERELL, M. HENNESSEY, P. and WALKER, D. *Sources close to the Prime Minister* Macmillan, 1984

CONGRESSIONAL QUARTERLY *Congressional Quarterly's guide to Congress* Congressional Quarterly, 2nd edn. 1976

CROSSMAN, R. H. *The diaries of a cabinet minister* 3 vols ed. Howard, Hamish Hamilton/Jonathan Cape, 1975–77

DAUBE, M. *How to run a pressure group* in *Marketing* October 1979, pp 75–77

ECKSTEIN, H. *Pressure group politics: the case of the British Medical Association* Allen and Unwin, 1960 op

ETZIONI, A. *The active society* Collier Macmillan, 1968 op

FINER, S. E. *Anonymous empire* Pall Mall Press, 1958 op

GORDON, C. ed. *Erskine May's parliamentary practice* Butterworths, 20th edn. 1983

GUSFIELD, J. *Symbolic crusade: status politics and the American Temperance Movement* Greenwood Press, 1963, 1980

HALL, P. *Diaries* ed. J. Goodwin, Hamish Hamilton, 1983

HAWTREY, S. C. and BARCLAY, H. M. *Abraham and Hawtrey's parliamentary dictionary* Butterworths, 3rd edn. 1970 op

Hollis press and public relations annual 1983–84 Hollis

Directories, 1983

HUSKISSON, M. *Outfoxed* M. Huskisson, 1983

KENNEDY, J. *To keep the lobbyists within bounds* in *New York Times Magazine* 19 February 1956

KOSS, S. *The rise and fall of the political press* 2 vols Hamish Hamilton, 1981–84

LOWE, P and GOYDER, J. *Environmental groups in politics* Allen and Unwin, 1983

MARSH, D. ed. *Pressure politics: interest groups in Britain* Junction Books, 1983 op

MCKENZIE, R. *British political parties* Heinemann, 1955 op

MCKENZIE, R. *Parties, pressure groups and the British political process* in KIMBER, R and RICHARDSON, J. J. eds. *Pressure groups in Britain: a reader* Dent, 1974

MICHELS, R. *Political parties: a sociological study of oligarchical tendencies and modern democracy* Free Press, 1966

MILIBAND, R. *Political power and social theory* Vol. 1 JAI Press, 1980

NOP *Animal issues and their influence on voting* NOP Market Research Ltd, April 1983

PORRITT, E. *The unreformed House of Commons: parliamentary representation before 1832* 2 vols (1902) USA: Kelley 1970

ROTH, A. *The business backgrounds of members of Parliament* Parliamentary Profiles, 1981

RYAN, M. *The acceptable pressure group: a case study of the Howard League for Penal Reform and Radical Alternatives to Prison* Saxon House, 1978

SCHOFIELD, M. *The strange case of pot* Pelican, 1971 op

SHIPLEY, P. ed. *Directory of pressure groups and representative associations* Bowker, 2nd edn. 1979

TAYLOR, P. *Smoke ring: the politics of tobacco* Bodley Head, 1984

THOMAS, R. H. *The politics of hunting* Gower, 1983

TRUMAN, D. *The governmental process* Greenwood Press, n.e. 1982

WHITEHOUSE, M. *A most dangerous woman?* Lion Publishing, 1982

WILSON, D. *Pressure: the A to Z of campaigning in Britain* Heinemann, 1984

WILSON, G. *Special interests and policymaking* Wiley, 1977 op

WOOTTON, G. *Pressure groups in Britain 1720–1790* Allen Lane, 1975 op

Official publications

Acceptance of outside appointments by crown servants: eighth report from the Treasury and Civil Service Committee Chmn. T. L. Higgins, HCP 302, 1983/84

Cannabis: report by the Advisory Committee on Drug Dependence Chmn. E. Wayne, Home Office, 1979

Land for housing Dept. of the Environment Draft Circular 2/161, 1983

Memorandum on structure and local plans and green belt Dept. of the Environment Draft Circular 2/162, 1983

Penal practice in a changing society Cmnd 645, 1959

Public and private funding of the arts House of Commons Committee on Education, Science and the Arts, HCP 239, 1981/82

Register of members interests on 7th February 1984 HCP 249, 1983/4

Royal Commission on the provision of legal services Chmn. H. Benson. Cmnd 7648, 1979

Programmes

BBC Television *Honourable members* 5 programmes on MPs, first broadcast BBC 2 1983

Index